How a Hashtag Changed the World lifts the curtain on a global movement and reveals stirring stories of a community that had an incalculable impact. Read it and be inspired.
Kristin Sherry
YouMap® Creator and bestselling author of YouMap

In this book, Anna and Nicole beautifully detail not only the history of the #LinkedInLocal movement, but also the core of why it captured the attention and hearts of so many in the business world that were looking for a place where they could truly belong. It is a must-read for any current or future leader.
Michaela Alexis
LinkedIn trainer, consultant and speaker

We all have ideas that have the potential to change the world. But how does that idea turn into a positive global social movement? The story of #LinkedInLocal is full of unexpected surprises and hope. This is the narrative that you want to follow if you have similar ambitions for both your local and global communities. It is the grounding that you need to prepare for the things you cannot change, and the motivation you need when you are faced with the things you can change.
Katrina Ramage
Founder, The Eye of the Storm

Cover design and photography by Mariona Grau
Typesetting by Caroline Goldsmith

HOW
A HASHTAG
CHANGED
THE
WORLD

Stories, Lessons and Reflections
from the #LinkedInLocal Movement

Anna McAfee and Nicole Johnston

To one of my
favourite authors!
Very Best wishes
Nicole J xxx

To the determined, passionate, dedicated and wonderful souls whose selfless efforts can and will change the world. May the force be with you!

Contents

Foreword

It was August of 2016 when I woke up completely energised by an idea that I knew could change lives.

I was compelled to bring some of my most intelligent, generous, thoughtful LinkedIn connections to a face-to-face event. I had learned from them by reading their brilliant content on the site. We'd engaged in deep discussions in the comments sections and via private message. I knew bringing them together would increase our learning opportunities exponentially.

The No Longer Virtual idea (NLV) was born that day, and the first event took place in Atlanta, Georgia, USA in February 2017 with 23 people meeting up for a two-day conference. During the debrief at end of the second day, we all agreed this was something that just had to happen again – preferably annually and in a central location.

Meeting each other face to face offered incredible learning opportunities as the session topics were relevant and well-facilitated. But it also created a tight-knit tribe of professionals that continue to support each other. We continue to share each other's content, brainstorm our biggest business challenges, and encourage each other to define our version of success and reach for it. The lesson was clear: beginning relationships online can be powerful, and meeting people face to face after developing a relationship online creates an extraordinary shift by building even greater trust and stronger connections.

Because of the success of No Longer Virtual, I immediately recognised the power and potential of #LinkedInLocal when I heard about it through Anna McAfee shortly after the first NLV in 2017. I co-hosted my first #LinkedInLocal in January 2018 in Berkeley, California. I had travelled from my home in Helena, Montana to visit family and I wanted to meet with some of my LinkedIn connections in the California area. I found three local connections to help me host an event and we set it up.

I started posting on LinkedIn about the upcoming event and my connection Curt Mercadante reached out to me. He was going to be in the area, visiting from South Carolina, and wanted to join us. Nearly 30 people who had never met in person gathered in a local brewery in Berkeley, California. They were mostly locals but there were a few of us from more distant states. That small group collected nearly $300 for a local non-profit – Rubicon Programs. It was magical.

#LinkedInLocal's founders created something extraordinary and relevant. It's especially important now, as our global community addresses an epidemic of loneliness, depression, and now a pandemic that limits our connections with other humans in even more significant ways.

Imagine what we can learn from this book that highlights the beauty and power of human connection? What Anna and Nicole have created is a source of inspiration for community building, authentic connection and a playbook for what networking can truly deliver: life changing relationships and experiences. Readers will be inspired by Anna's brilliant idea, generosity, and ability to enlist others in her #LinkedInLocal story, to reach beyond the keyboard in their professional relationships and create an inspiring story of their own.

Sarah Elkins
Founder, No Longer Virtual events
Author of *Your Stories Don't Define You, How You Tell Them Will*

Part One: Origins

Introduction

Let us start, quite simply, with a river.

Rivers begin life with a source – melting snow, a glacier, a spring or a lake. From there a tiny flow runs downstream and meets other sources of water. It gathers pace, growing larger until the flow becomes a river.

Rivers are enabled by gravity. The steeper the slope the faster they flow, and then their energy grows. On their way downwards the water shapes the landscape by wearing away rock and carving out a network of valleys. It is never straight or defined – it finds a natural flow.

Rivers often form rapids, or waterfalls, depending on their course and the landscape around them. A river can meet flatter land where it will lose some momentum and its speed slows. The river then widens and takes a more meandering route.

Some rivers are strong all year round depending on how much water flows into them. Others flow seasonally. Some are small – but no less important. Others – are so large that they can span entire countries or continents.

Eventually most rivers empty out into the sea, but their journeys have not only carved out the landscape but also shaped the worlds of the people and animals who live alongside these tributaries.

For centuries, they have been the lifeblood for human society. Rivers have provided humans not just with water but also with food. Humans have been drawn to rivers as ideal places to put down roots, to grow crops and build communities. Rivers have enabled mass exploration and, eventually, opportunities for trade. Rivers not only provide a link between communities up and downstream, they provide a means for stories and ideas to travel.

I think of #LinkedInLocal as a river. Just as rivers have been critical to the development of many communities, #LinkedInLocal has become a force critical to the development of so many people and their local communities.

It was a simple idea. It began as a trickle, fed by other sources and influences. The early adopters of the movement were the small streams that came together and made the river larger and stronger. It then began to gather pace to create real momentum.

It gave many a sense of purpose, a place to belong, a world in which to explore ideas and have conversations. It put real faces to online names. It led to more 'hello's and smiles, instead of comments and likes.

This book is my experience of the first two years of starting, leading and managing the global #LinkedInLocal movement. An idea, propelled across the world, that touched the lives of people in 650 cities, in 92 countries in its first two years. In that time I estimate, based on the number of events and attendees, that it has directly impacted between 300,000-500,000 people. It remains LinkedIn's longest running and most popular hashtag.

This book is largely a collection of the stories that flooded my inbox and social media newsfeeds for the first two years of the #LinkedInLocal movement. They are the stories of the people behind their LinkedIn profiles – what they believe in and what they stand for. These are the stories I decided couldn't remain in one person's inbox for no one but me to see and reflect upon. They needed to be told, shared and, most importantly, they needed to be considered.

This is a book about human beings. It is a book about tolerance and a reflection of where we find ourselves in the world right now – 2020 and beyond. I hope it will provide some insight as to how we can use social media for good – how we can bend and shape its purpose to meet our own human needs and the needs of our wider society. I hope it can provide something like a blueprint for how communities can help build a more accepting, tolerant and understanding society. And I hope it just might help you feel better about human beings and their intentions. Whatever you get from this, please know that this is not just my story and it's not just the stories of the people featured in this book, but it is also the beginning of the story for many thousands more to come.

It can be the beginning of your story too.

The Idea

'#LinkedInLocals stand out from other events because of the atmosphere and types of people coming along – they are less stiff, don't force their business cards on you and are more interested in getting to know your story.'
Dr. Natalia Wiechowski, speaker at #LinkedInLocal Dubai, Berlin and Warsaw

'#LinkedInLocal Navi Mumbai was built on the philosophy of inclusivity and creating strong connections. It has become a family rather than a networking event.'
Kalpesh and Shalaka Raichura, #LinkedInLocal Navi Mumbai, India

Ideas can come from anywhere, from a whim, a tiny spark or from what seems like nothing at all. In the words of Victor Hugo, 'There is one thing stronger than all the armies in the world, and that is an idea whose time has come.'

It was April 2017 and my life had changed beyond recognition. Since 2002 I had enjoyed a career in the recruitment industry, starting in Glasgow, Scotland before relocating to Coffs Harbour, Australia in 2012. During that time I was a business manager for two start-up recruitment businesses and, as is often the case in new businesses, I had become accustomed to extremely busy days and holding a high level of responsibility. The pace was fast and changing. In both businesses, I somehow became the go-to person for IT issues, staff inductions, changing light bulbs and everything in between. I loved it – the people, the challenges, the variety and pace of the industry.

Fast forward to 2017, I was now the mother of a three-year-old and a one-year-old, and my days couldn't have been more different. There was a greater sense of responsibility, but the pace was a lot slower and very routine driven. But, more than that, I was provided less of an opportunity to be part of a team and to meet a variety of people. I enjoyed motherhood but I found it isolating at times. The parenting community can be a supportive one but also one fraught with judgement. I was blessed with many great friends who were fellow parents, and a supportive husband, but I found socialising with new parents to be an onerous experience at times, due to high expectations. This, coupled with sleep deprivation, isn't always the best environment to feel a sense of self and belonging. I was itching to get back to a more authentic social experience, with more than one topic of conversation – to an environment that felt more real and more supportive. Three years into motherhood and I was – quite simply – in need of more adult conversation. I am an only child and no stranger to isolation and, whilst my upbringing did mean I was used to my own company, it also meant I was experienced in being proactive in getting to know others.

The career opportunities at the time for me did not feel endless. I lived in a regional Australian city where job opportunities, especially those for part-time work, were scarce. I was not yet ready to commit to full-time employment as I wanted to maintain care of my children and only work three to four days per week. Setting up my own small business seemed like the ideal option, specialising in areas that I knew – training, IT support, marketing and social media. I was largely focused on the local market – businesses directly around me – and I started looking for ways in which I could establish a business that utilised my knowledge, provided flexibility and was feasible financially. My business idea was based around helping local businesses in Coffs Harbour with their online presence. Many laid their priorities with platforms like Facebook, Twitter or Instagram but the platform with which I had the most experience – LinkedIn – was often a second or even a third thought.

LinkedIn had been the source of a huge change in recruitment. As part of my previous role, I was responsible for IT and staff training, and that meant training a lot of recruiters to use LinkedIn for sourcing candidates, marketing, expanding their networks and building trust online. I was drawn to LinkedIn for its focused content often based on personal development and the sharing of ideas, as well as its supportive community of users. It was different to other social media platforms in that there was little sharing of frivolities, it was more purposeful and presented a lot of career opportunities.

LinkedIn was an effective tool and platform for so many people. I witnessed first-hand the digital disruption as the uptake in the platform grew. The recruitment industry was shaken up by the move from inputted curriculum vitae ('CV') recruitment data, to live job data on LinkedIn. From that moment on I became a fan, albeit a fairly quiet one. Being an introvert I was more comfortable as a social listener, scrolling through and reading other people's content. I had yet to build my confidence enough to share my own thoughts and ideas. However, having always been in an internal role as a trainer and manager rather than in client facing roles up until 2017, I wasn't using LinkedIn to its full potential. In my recruitment career I was training others to use the platform, but not using it a lot myself to network with clients. More than just being a recruitment tool, it provided users an opportunity to connect with other users all over the world, to collaborate, build influence and demonstrate thought leadership.

Many introverts by nature can sometimes feel less intimidated networking behind a screen than meeting people in person. As a self-identified introvert, LinkedIn was filling a void in my life – it gave me a network of humans who were open, honest, supportive and willing to listen. It was like a window back to my old life and career and, now I was trying to find some balance between motherhood and that career, I was hooked. Here I found interesting articles and posts on how people had overcome career challenges. They were sharing their stories about mental health or burnout. Thought leaders were offering advice on how to further develop your skills and mindset. These were human stories, told well, with emotion and authenticity. And the people sharing them seemed to be motivated by something other than trying to make a quick sale.

LinkedIn was where I felt at home so that was where I started. I needed to meet people, develop relationships and grow my own brand, and the platform seemed the best way to do this. I reconnected with the platform, refreshed my profile and began by reaching out to interesting connections locally. LinkedIn is a truly international community but, for me, it made sense to start local. Building up a business meant connecting with people and gaining their trust. Rarely do people see a link and buy without hesitation. Credibility is important and that is easier to create when you can meet face to face. I was keen to build a business that would support my local community. My need for more face to face human interaction would also be satisfied, so focusing on a local network made a lot of sense.

Whilst reaching out to people locally I could see a huge diversity in both the background and professions of some local users. It was incredibly easy to connect with these local users and get to know them and their businesses via LinkedIn content. I was starting to build up a strong and supportive network of friends and they were right here in my own community. I met up with a few of my new contacts one-to-one. Like me, many were working from home, juggling families and other commitments and looking to connect in a way that wasn't entirely geared towards the hard sell.

In April 2017 LinkedIn underwent a major platform

redesign. I was curious so I signed up for a free trial of the Sales Navigator programme. Sales Navigator is a LinkedIn premium subscription that crucially gives visibility of users activity, specifically those that had posted content in the previous 30 days. After conducting a postcode search in April 2017, I discovered some interesting statistics. In my local city of Coffs Harbour, within a 50 km radius there were approximately 23,000 users and 289 of these were active at the time. Only 289 active? Was that all? Really? Only 12%? I'd exposed a problem that many LinkedIn users can sympathise with. There are so many LinkedIn users (660 million at the end of 2019) but it was widely known back in 2017 that the percentage of the platform that were active was somewhere between 24–25%.

LinkedIn has a reputation that is changing but many of its users still view the platform as beneficial solely for the purpose of recruitment. Many users only come back to LinkedIn when seeking work, perhaps every two to three years. Also, being a work platform, there are so many dormant accounts. Users set up profiles whilst working at a company, then abandon them when they move on, but those accounts remain open. Having access to active user lists on Sales Navigator was powerful and, crucially, helped me understand who best to connect with and where there were gaps.

Coffs Harbour is a small city in New South Wales, Australia. It is a city with a population of just 76,000, and whilst there were almost eight daily flights to the cities of Sydney and Melbourne, much of the business community depends on the support of fellow local businesses. Regional and even larger isolated cities (by geography) tend to be reliant on the support of one another. Local support and bonds are strong as our customer base and networks are often smaller when compared to larger regions and cities.

In May 2017 I posted the following question on LinkedIn:

> 'Apparently there are 23,000 users locally, and only 289 are active. Coffs Harbour, surely we can do better than that?'

A few comments followed – about LinkedIn not really being 'a thing' in Australia, and a number talking about the lack of engagement. Then there was a comment from Nicole K Martin: 'Well, if it's so small, why don't we all meet up?'

It was such a simple idea. And I thought, 'Why not?' LinkedIn provided a great, international platform with a community of diverse people willing to share and connect, but no features to encourage local engagement. For residents of smaller cities across the world, and especially in Australia, there isn't even a search field for their city and users could only search by state or region. In a world where it's so easy to connect globally, the need to connect with people in your immediate environment can often seem irrelevant for some LinkedIn users which would explain the lack of local engagement on the platform. But what if we took it offline?

I sat with the idea for a week. It was an obvious solution but would it work? Would any of those 289 active local accounts show up? I cared enough about the idea to give it a shot. Even if only five people came, surely it would be worthwhile for those that did?

On 22nd May 2017 I put the following post up on LinkedIn with little expectation.

'Coffs Harbour, I'm organising a LinkedIn Local catch up. Come along next Friday and meet your LinkedIn connections in person. Feel free to share with your local connections. #LinkedInLocal'

It was an achingly simple idea. It got 22 likes and 37 comments – it could hardly be considered viral. Social media posts are transient and remain in our consciousness for only a few minutes – maybe a few days if they are thought-provoking. But a few will linger in people's minds and change human behaviour.

Before I clicked publish on the post, I added the #LinkedInLocal hashtag as an afterthought. Why did I add the hashtag? In March 2017, I'd written my first article on LinkedIn in response to a question posed by Mark Williams in his *LinkedInformed* podcast: 'How can we better engage with millennials on LinkedIn?' I explained in my article that a very simple answer to this question could be hashtags, given their extensive use on other more millennially-engaged social media platforms. I think that was the reason for adding the hashtag. I really believed that hashtags could encourage participation. They have the power to spark movements, activate people and, every once in a while, change human behaviour. The hashtag #MeToo became a real call for cultural change and is synonymous with something beyond the posts. The

ALS Association's #IceBucketChallenge activated millions of people to raise money and use social media to do something good for the world. But, as I clicked publish, I couldn't possibly know that this post would change my life, my career and that of so many others around the world.

The response from the local community on the site was good. Several users tagged other users they knew in the comments, people I was not yet connected to. Many asked how they could help and were very open to the idea of meeting in person. The first #LinkedInLocal event took place a week later in Coffs Harbour on the 2nd of June 2017. Fifteen people arrived to enjoy a coffee together, one crisp winter morning in a small city in Australia. There was no charge to attend the event, and no agenda except to meet – face to face – and get to know the people behind the LinkedIn profiles. It was about connecting at a human level, enriching the online network offline and learning more about one another – something that is sometimes only possible through conversation, rather than a slightly-too-polished online profile.

The diversity of people who came and the ensuing conversations were incredible. In the words of Kellie Pearce who attended the event – and many more after – 'this great initiative brought a diverse group of people together with an initial aim of just getting to meet like-minded people in an informal setting. Not only did that succeed but we were able to learn more about our community at large and learn from each other.' I was so relieved that the event was a success and was immediately inspired to do more.

During that first meeting we discussed local business issues, social media, workplace diversity, early morning starts, artistic interests outside of work, strengthening support networks and, encouragingly, how we could develop the group and grow.

Although I was pleased with the response to our first meetup in Coffs Harbour, I was totally unprepared for the response to the post from further afield. The post hadn't exactly gone viral, but it had been seen by people beyond Coffs Harbour. Alexandra (Alex) Galviz, a LinkedIn personal branding and strategy coach and graduate development trainer, commented about wanting to start something for her own community in London. Alex was someone I had connected with in the months prior, inspired by her authentic content and her lessons shared from a quarter-life crisis and travelling through India. Shortly after Alex's response, Erik Eklund, a brilliant storyteller, speaker and facilitator based in Brussels at the time commented and said he'd look to get something happening in his city. Erik and I were not connected at the time – he saw the post via a mutual connection. Finally, Swish Goswami, a serial entrepreneur and UN Youth Ambassador in New York City joined the conversation a few weeks later. Swish posted a lot of content about taking an unconventional approach to business which really appealed to me and he and I had connected just prior to me posting that first message. Within hours of that first #LinkedInLocal post, a chain reaction had started. These people were to become the different parts of a dynamic co-creation team.

Erik held his first event on 7th June 2017 with 15 people and the intention of showcasing some of the entrepreneurial businesses in Brussels. They even included a specially created cocktail for the event. Even with the relatively small number of attendees the event was lively. As we would come to find in other cities who started events early, the small numbers meant people really felt they were able to interact and get to know one another, and that was different to many other networking events they had attended.

After his first event, Erik, reflecting on why he was so drawn to the idea, said, 'For me it's just taking what's online offline and really connecting. At the beginning of 2017, I gave myself a goal that I wanted to meet at least 25 of my LinkedIn contacts in real life, wherever they were in the world. I came to realise, through my coaching, that people are really reluctant to get out there and meet people. And I started to tell them that it's worthwhile investing time in those kinds of connections without even *knowing* what type of objective you have for doing it. Just meeting people. #LinkedInLocal for me was really about putting a personality behind the profile, behind the social media post.'

Alex explains that, prior to #LinkedInLocal, 'I was going to a lot of networking events as a new business owner, trying to meet other business owners and find some form of support network. People who were like-minded and could help each other out. Instead, I found these events where people were shoving business cards down my throat, trying to get something from me. I just didn't really like their environment and the atmosphere. I wasn't finding the right people to connect with. I was less interested in doing business with other business owners and more interested in developing a community, a group of people or a support network of people that were interested in growth and development and helping each other.'

'When I first saw Anna's #LinkedInLocal post in my newsfeed, my first thought was "This looks familiar" because whilst I was not doing the group version, I was doing one-to-one – taking conversations offline – and I'd hashtagged it #virtualtoreality. I was sharing stories and snippets of the people I was meeting. So, when I saw what Anna was doing, it seemed like the natural evolution of what I was already doing. And I liked the idea of bringing a group of people together. I've always been someone that likes getting together and sitting around a table, having dinner or drinks, exchanging conversations and stories. So, I instantly thought, why not? This looks like something that I would be interested in getting involved with.'

Alex held her first event in London on 22nd June 2017. She said, 'For me it was really about getting people to come without the masks from work, without titles on their business cards and really coming with an open mind, willing to explore, experience and connect with others. That sense of connection and facilitating that connection, for me, was really, really important.'

Although Swish and I connected before my first #LinkedInLocal post, he'd already been playing with the idea of a meetup when he moved to New York in June 2017. He said, 'I'd seen some friends on

YouTube running meetups when they were visiting cities, and thought, hey, if they're doing a meetup and they don't have that big of a following… I had a decent following on LinkedIn and thought maybe I should do a meetup in New York.'

'The first meetup was in Washington Square Park. Twenty people came out and I almost cried. It was very humbling to see people come out. What I learned very quickly about the meetups was that they were never about me. I thought, going in, that people would come because of the organisers and expect facilitated conversation. But what I saw immediately was how naturally people were talking to each other. That's where it hit me – these meetups aren't just about one person. It's about bringing the entire community where they connect with each other and hopefully grow together.'

So the first four #LinkedInLocal events had been kickstarted, establishing new networks in London, Brussels, New York City and little Coffs Harbour.

Bringing people together was not a new idea nor was it a unique one – it was only innovative at that time because so few people were doing it in a world of *online* social networking. Its appeal globally was in its simplicity and in what it stood for in terms of values. The events were open and accessible to everyone, strictly for no profit and pitch-free with no hidden agenda. They were designed to simply bring people together and allow attendees to get to know the people behind the profiles. It wasn't just about connecting professionals for the sole reason of doing business or generating leads, but to meet – face to face – share common ground and create a supportive environment for one another. It would later activate a sense of belonging amongst so many humans and, for many organisers of these events, a deep sense of purpose.

As Elizabeth Gilbert explains in her book *Big Magic*, creativity is not just creative pursuits such as writing or painting, but innovative thinking and the understanding that the sharing of ideas and collaboration is what makes humanity thrive. Gilbert asserts that there are millions of ideas floating around, just looking for the right human collaborator. This struck me as especially poignant given what we had sparked here. I have lost count of the number of times people have said to me in conversation, 'I had this idea', or 'I've tried this before but have never had the time to follow through with it.' Sometimes you just need a push and that can sometimes come in the form of a moment in time or a collaborator – and sometimes both.

In 2017, the world had spent the better part of ten years increasingly existing online. The digital world was changing the ways in which we were networking, connecting and doing business. Millennials had only known the workplace and networking from a digital perspective. As inflated marketing messages and fake news expanded into our inboxes and social feeds, many people were beginning to seek out something else. It wasn't just me who felt the need for something different, something more real.

In his 2005 Stanford Commencement Speech, Steve Jobs shared the following:

'You can't connect the dots looking forward; you can only connect them looking backwards. So, you have to trust that the dots will somehow connect in your future.'

For me, at that moment, 'the dots connected'. My love of LinkedIn, my circumstances and my passion for starting conversations and supporting other people were all to align at the right time and, crucially, with the *right* individual collaborators – people who had the energy to get behind it. The idea had always been floating around but it needed the right people to bring the idea to life globally. Things were about to change.

The Beginning of a Movement

'#LinkedInLocal captures the fabric of authentic human interaction that slices through titles, and prestige and makes us all people exchanging ideas, interactions and value without any expectation of something in return.'
Koehler Slagel, #LinkedInLocal
Lexington, Kentucky, USA

'When we started #LinkedInLocal in Fort Lauderdale the reason I said yes was because of the whole concept of connecting with people for who they really are, and not for what I want to get or gain from them. It's amazing, and in today's society I think that there is a huge need for connecting with people in a real and honest way, as opposed to just connecting because you want to get something in return.'
Evelyn Andrade, #LinkedInLocal
Fort Lauderdale, Florida, USA

Derek Sivers gave a very powerful TED talk in 2014 called *How To Start A Movement*. In a three minute clip, available online, he explains how movements begin and the crucial elements that are required. He shows the audience video footage of a man dancing on his own, away from the crowd, at a festival. His movements are strange and could be expected to be met with ridicule. But instead he is joined by another man – his 'first follower'. Sivers acknowledges wryly, that it is the 'first follower' who turns the first dancer into 'a leader'. He says that it takes courage to both be the 'first dancer' and also the first 'follower' and both are important. In the video, the two dancers are joined by another dancer and then another. Soon, says Sivers, we have momentum and eventually 'we have a movement'.

Sivers goes on to say: 'If you are a version of the shirtless, dancing guy – all alone – remember the importance of nurturing your first few followers as equals, making everything clearly about the movement, not you … Leadership is over-glorified. Yes – it started with the shirtless guy, and he'll get all the credit – but you saw what really happened, it was the first follower that transformed a lone nut into a leader. There is no movement without the first follower. We're told we all need to be leaders, but that would be really ineffective. The best way to create a movement, if you really care, is to courageously follow and show others how to follow. When you find a lone nut doing something great, have the guts to be the first person to stand up and join in.'

In the case of #LinkedInLocal, there were three 'first followers': Alex, Erik and Swish. They made the hashtag a movement and when that happened the movement wasn't just about me anymore but all of us.

Sivers' TED talk explains exactly what happened with the #LinkedInLocal movement kickstarters.

#LinkedinLocal would have been a blip in the LinkedIn newsfeed were it not for the courage and leadership of Alex, Erik and Swish.

We embraced each other as equals. We shared experiences of our first events. And it was them who courageously showed others how to follow. I was not a leader without them, there would be no movement had they not chosen to follow in the first place. There was Alex with her authentic values and warmth, Erik with his skills of connecting and his energy, and Swish with his genuine nature and growth mindset. If #LinkedInLocal was a living being and I was the centre – it was only able to grow with the help of Alex's far-reaching and open arms, with Erik's passion that gave the idea legs and with the expertise of Swish who gave it viral wings.

After the first events in each of our respective cities, the four of us began chatting to share ideas, explore the future and its possibilities. How were we going to grow these offline communities? What values would we follow? And how could we support each other from afar? We started posting content about the events on LinkedIn and more people expressed interest in also getting involved. A common goal we started to see was people looking for help in keeping consistency, in managing a community not just an event, and in creating something that added value to attendees and was different to other networking evetns. So, in the interest of keeping some consistency city to city we established the following core values:

- Collaboration, not competition
- Authentic, always

- Diverse and inclusive
- Respectful of one another

This was our first step towards curating the movement. We established that events would always be pitch-free to ensure that we were respectful and created an environment where people felt that they belonged. Events had to be strictly not-for-profit, either run for free or, if a fee needed to be charged to cover costs, any surplus proceeds were to go to a charity. Attendees were encouraged to leave their business cards at home, to come along as themselves and get to know one another at a human level.

In Coffs Harbour we had started running events monthly. The second event in July 2017 had 20 people in attendance and word was spreading. Throughout the latter half of 2017 the events would attract between 18–25 people and attendees were strengthening online relationships by meeting offline. At the same time, we were starting to communicate more regularly with each other online – interacting and boosting each other's posts and articles.

Alex in London and Erik in Brussels also started running regular events, which were increasing in popularity and getting positive feedback. Swish co-hosted a meetup in Shanghai in July 2017 with a contact of his, John Patrick Mullin, and posted a group photo of the event. The post reached 1.4 million LinkedIn users and eventually caught the attention of Jeff Weiner, LinkedIn's CEO at the time. Weiner commented about perhaps thinking of developing some tools to support users in their meetups and tagged Ryan Roslansky, the Senior Vice President of Product at LinkedIn at that time. We'd got their attention.

Rumblings were starting around the world. People were using the hashtag. More cities started to see #LinkedInLocal events. In North America and Europe many were waiting until the summer was over to launch their first events but people were starting to get organised.

In September 2017, something happened that aligned the stars for what would be a world changing movement: the release of LinkedIn native video. This allowed users to upload video direct to the platform from mobile or desktop. Previously video could only be shared via external links to websites such as YouTube or Vimeo and the algorithm pushed these posts from receiving high-viewing numbers. After the launch, native video became the king of content and those who participated in video creation in those early days were about to see ideas and careers take off.

That September, I shared a simple face-to-camera video about starting #LinkedInLocal and the idea behind it. 'I believe we have a deep need for human connection,' I said, 'not just in business but in life. Social media has blurred the lines affecting the way we communicate, the way we sell, the way we do business and largely the way we think. Getting back to basics, taking our connections offline, meeting them face to face and shaking hands is what people are really craving. In many facets of life, we are craving community, we may think "global" but "local" is central to who we are.'

Swish shared a video using footage he had taken at the earlier Shanghai event. He talked about the opportunities that LinkedIn presented in terms of building influence. 'If you, right now, decide to start posting – start sharing a bit of your journey out there – you're still early. There aren't many people who have figured out the amount of traction you can get on LinkedIn – how many opportunities are out there.'

In the footage from the Shanghai event, John Patrick Mullin, an investment banker, speaker and writer, shared, 'This is the offline engagement we have been talking about, actually getting people to get out there and meet each other.'

Alex shared a video of another event held on a sweltering London evening on a Thames river boat. In it she explains 'I know a lot of you know each other online and you are keen to meet those people face to face. At the end of the day it's so important who you surround yourself with. Especially when you are on the same wavelength – you're talking about challenging ideas, and you gain so much from it. You connect with humans when you talk about the interests that you share, the passions that you share and that's what matters. We are humans after all. It's so important that we connect with each other even when those relationships have been built virtually.'

Erik shared a video from a vibrant event in Barcelona. 'Take a look at yourself,' he asked 'Why are you doing things? Because you have a label stamped on your forehead? Or because you have a heart full of desires? Some of you are going for your dreams right now, some of you aren't. You would like to. Right now, I'm just trying out this concept to help all of you – and myself – to get out there and do something about it… In one room we today have 17 languages, and I'll bet in this one room we have more than 17 interests, desires, passions, or beliefs. Just try and go personal first… If I could just ask you to tell the room one thing about you that you normally don't share, what would you say?'

The videos shared from Shanghai, London and Barcelona really captured the energy and soul of the events. They didn't just feature the organisers either – they showed the diversity of the people coming together. Set to music, they featured scenes from the city, contemporary venues, people interacting and interviews with attendees. Attendees shared what they felt was so valuable to them about these events, and what they had gained or learned from LinkedIn that they could share with others. They talked about the people they'd met, their own vulnerabilities, their passions, their aspirations and how the interactions had helped them develop personally and professionally.

Suddenly these events were brought to life in the newsfeed through video, for all of the world to watch. Judd Laurie who attended #LinkedInlocal events in Buffalo in New York, USA, told us, 'I screen captured a video with my phone in one hand and recorded the event with my camera in the other. I ended up making a promo video out of it and within about 12 hours of the event, it went viral. View rates were between 2,500 and 3,500 per hour. It reached about 80,000 views inside of three days. I was blown away and literally thought it was a glitch. This all happened within 24 hours of having my third baby. I was literally uploading the video as I was heading out the door to go to the hospital. Watching the numbers at the same time as waiting in the delivery room was insane.'

Increasing visibility due to video meant that our inboxes and newsfeeds were almost instantly flooded with messages: 'I need this in my city'; 'Can you help me get started?'; 'How can I replicate the success of your event?' and 'Is there a way for me to learn from others?'

Alex recalls, 'I was one of the first to have video content at a time where video was still quite new on LinkedIn. The video was able to show people what those events were about in a visual format and proved that these were not ordinary networking events – it was more of a community developing. What I was trying to create and build was community. When we talked about no "sales pitching" or business cards – it was great to be able to explain that visually as well, through interviewing people that were there – it provided a lot more context for viewers.'

The slope of the river had tilted dramatically. The desire for real connection – to be at events that were not about selling, to be seen as a human and not a job title or business card – was real and it was being felt on a global scale. The people expressing an interest in bringing these events to their city – to find a way to truly connect – were from such diverse backgrounds, religions, cultures and continents. The sheer demand and volume of requests for help from around the world meant we had to do something.

So we, the four founders, put our heads together. LinkedIn didn't offer much in terms of technical support. The site had previously had an events area as part of the platform but had shut it down in 2012 due to lack of use. Just five years later this showed that the need for event facilities was there after all. But we'd need to develop our own resources.

Erik put together a guide, in the form of a PDF document that could be shared via email, on demand. This was largely the starting point for many hosts in these early few months. And we added the phrase and hashtag #connectinghumans to our online communications. It was an idea previously used by Erik, a simple phrase to help share the movement and it was adopted quickly by early hosts. The guide outlined the 'what, how and why' that enabled the beginning of the community-building process we were to establish. And it was this guide that opened the gates to finding the right hosts who really embodied the spirit of the idea.

As more events began happening, more videos and posts were shared using the hashtag on LinkedIn. These posts acted as catalysts for growth. A host would post about their event and people from their network would comment and ask whether they knew about any events closer to their own location. We would often run through lists of these comments on hosts' profiles responding to tag in the host for that user's specific location. This was how most of the initial host introductions were made and how the community started to grow further. The movement was self-perpetuating in this way, where it wasn't just the founders inspiring others. Many followers joined the movement because they saw someone who they knew already involved and that helped them to feel encouraged to be a part of it as well. In this way the flow of the river expanded and provided a link between communities up and downstream.

Our goal was to find a way of curating the community – finding the right hosts who would share our values was crucial to its success. We weren't looking for those who would just piggyback on the success of the hashtag and turn events into a sales pitch. We were looking for those who understood it was about the community and not about their own agenda. By the end of November 2017 #LinkedInLocal events were happening in 60 global cities with 40 more planning their first event. We realised that the guide wasn't enough. With multiple messages arriving in multiple inboxes and LinkedIn not providing the tools we needed for managing this kind of community and the number of enquiries growing fast – we realised that what we really needed was a website.

We started to put the feelers out about creating a digital home with the help of Brian Almeida – an entrepreneur based in Brampton, Canada, and one of the early hosts that helped mentor new hosts in Canada to get their own local offline communities started. We looked at domains, and found that www.linkedinlocal.com was already registered to a LinkedIn user based in Liverpool, England. He had a similar idea several years previously but had yet to execute it. We had a conversation in October 2017, and whilst respectful of our idea and values, he wasn't keen to be involved and wanted to retain rights to the domain. We then learned that LinkedIn's branding rules stated the user agreement prohibited the launch of a website with the word LinkedIn in the URL. We began searching for alternatives and finally landed on www.linkedlocally.com.

Like many LinkedIn users, up until #LinkedInLocal launched, Ryan Troll, a product designer and creative entrepreneur based in Washington DC, had not been especially active on the platform. 'Back in October 2017 I had decided that I needed to diversify the ways that I was meeting people and finding new work,' Ryan recalls. 'So, at the time, I was thinking that I had to figure out how to get more traction on LinkedIn. Up until then I'd been the person who updates their profile once a year and posts a couple of drab articles. That was about it. And so I remember logging on and straight away, Anna showed up in my feed. I remember reading one of her posts about #LinkedInLocal and my very first thought was, "Okay, this sounds cool".'

So, it was out of the blue, in October 2017, that I received a message from Ryan and it was one that impacted everyone involved in #LinkedInLocal. 'Hey Anna, I love the concept of #LinkedInLocal and recently attended one in DC. Can I put together a free website for you?' So entered Ryan, our fifth co-founder. He was instantly a great collaborator, idea driver and technical implementor for the movement and he was what we needed to really grow the community further. As the energy behind the river grew, carving the landscape and providing for so many communities, Ryan was able to add to this energy, keeping it on course and helping to channel it in the right direction.

Structure, Synergy and Scale

'We were one of the first handful of #LinkedInLocal events in 2017, and the first to hit 100 attendees. That said bigger isn't always better when it comes to connection. Connection is something that has always been part of what I love to do. I love to hear the stories of connection, the collaborations, partnerships and opportunities.'
Jo Saunders, #LinkedInLocal Perth, Australia

'Within a couple of months I have been able to grow my business through conversations that would not have happened had there not been two things: the LinkedIn platform and #LinkedInLocal. I endorse the heart of this movement. The growth that has occurred because of the simple focus on kindness, caring and sharing has touched my Caribbean island and, by extension, me.'
Engel Jones, #LinkedInLocal
Trinidad and Tobago

Our resources were limited and the budget to build a website was minimal, but we had a group of passionate volunteers and it was enough to ensure the community could grow and expand digitally. The website was built in one weekend, on a free WordPress template, by Ryan. This was to be #LinkedInLocal's first digital home outside of the LinkedIn platform itself. Its aim was to answer a few simple questions from the list of those that we were asked most frequently by people getting in touch:

How do I find events in my city and get involved?
How do I find events in the cities I travel to?
Where can I find information about what's involved?
How can I become a host?
Will you help me get started?
How can I meet other hosts and share ideas?

The website created an easily shareable resource that helped people to gain access to this information.

Ryan explains, 'We organised the launch [of the Wordpress site] in December 2017. The rockets fired up and we started giving it a home. As simple as that might sound, it was very impactful to help people understand what #LinkedInLocal was about and in helping the idea spread.'

Using the website, hosts were able to list their event locations, dates and topics, linking back to their LinkedIn profile so people could get in touch. The ticket collection still took place on other sites such as Eventbrite, so we had no visibility of the number of attendees per event, only the number of events actually taking place. However, at that time it was enough. People were able to look up what was going on in their region and get some basic information. More than that, people who were interested in becoming hosts of events themselves could use the website to book a video conference call and talk to someone who could walk them through the core values of #LinkedInLocal, how to set events up and build their own local community.

At the time of the website launch, the movement was still increasing in momentum. We had more and more people interested in setting up #LinkedInLocal events in their own locations. The founders were doing most of the one-to-one calls with new hosts and that was taking up a lot of time and energy. It got to the point where we simply just couldn't meet the demand of one-to-one and so began running group video calls for new hosts. Up to six prospective hosts could attend, and the website was extremely helpful in scheduling this.

The mentoring calls helped people understand what was involved in building a local community and running events, and gave them a chance to ask us questions. During these calls we talked about the origins of the movement, its values and the core intention to connect LinkedIn users beyond their profiles. We gave advice on event management, promotion, suitable topics for themed events, sponsors and finding speakers. We shared stories of previous successful launches to give an idea as to what had worked well so people could learn from others' successes. We also gave guidance on use of the hashtag and the name – whilst making it clear that the LinkedIn logo could not be used to promote events as this was not allowed. We encouraged people to form teams with co-hosts in their local area and reach out to other hosts in surrounding towns and cities, making online introductions to them. The calls were designed to provide information but by sharing the core values – not-for-profit, pitch-free, inclusive and collaborative – they were also an opportunity to pre-screen hosts and ascertain those who were simply looking to start events for their own self-promotion. Although these pre-screening stages were largely done on our own instincts and we were trusting our hosts to uphold the values of the movement there were some individuals who joined calls and realised this wasn't for them. The calls were a way to support others joining the movement but also to ensure the community was curated and the values were upheld. After the calls, those hosts still interested and ready to get engaged with our value system were provided with website login details, written guides and access to the host community – the groups we set up to help hosts connect with one another and share ideas.

There were a number of rogue hosts – those who set up events with their own intentions without contacting others in the host community. Those that we became aware of, we tried to contact and integrate into the movement – letting them know there were resources available to help them and a community to support them. Many took up our offer but those that didn't never really hosted for long.

Our record keeping at the time of the website launch also needed to improve. At that early stage, what would become the host database was simply scribbled notes in my diary, my notepads or information held in my own mind. I still have almost illegible notebooks with details of who I spoke to and when. In those notebooks are lists of names, locations, who they needed to be introduced to, or where they were planning to travel to. We wanted people to collaborate on events and not run competing events in the same city. We preferred that hosts were local to the city they were hosting in or to work with some local hosts if visiting. Pop-up events were good but local hosts were in a better position to organise future events and really build up a community rather than offering a one-off.

When the website went live in mid-December – a traditionally quiet time of year – it nevertheless opened the floodgates and we quickly realised we had a very hungry community on our hands. With the website, interested individuals had a place where they could book themselves onto a call without having to make an individual request via LinkedIn. Call spaces filled up fast – a lot faster than our LinkedIn requests had been coming in. The website was getting approximately 3,000 unique visits per month in those first few months. The website not only eased the pressure on our overstuffed inboxes but it also gave the movement and the hashtag a legitimacy that a web presence can provide and that only accelerated the growth of people getting in touch.

At the time of the web launch we had almost 200 hosts worldwide. Alex, Erik, Swish and I split the world into regions geographically each covering enquiries and calls with the part of the globe closest to our own locations. But the other founders were relying on the same ad hoc record keeping as I was at that stage, so effective communication between the four of us was hard. We relied on a WhatsApp chat that never slept due to our four different time zones in order to share information but, with the growing number of enquiries, we needed a better system. The website at least enabled those existing hosts to register somewhere and improved our information sharing and administration as the community grew.

The prominence of the hashtag on LinkedIn was responsible for a lot of the traffic but we came to realise that it was more direct word of mouth – people just talking to each other – that was allowing people to find us at such a rate. It never occurred to us to trademark the name at that stage – still being very aware of LinkedIn's terms of service – but it became quickly apparent that some sort of brand was being created.

As we launched the new website, we also created the host community – a digital space for hosts to meet, share ideas and gain support for their events. The host community initially communicated through a LinkedIn group, but then moved to a Slack group. We found the functionality of Slack improved engagement and also gave us the opportunity to create sub-groups for different geographical regions where people could find each other more easily.

The host community became central to so many hosts meeting one another, getting support and sharing ideas. New hosts felt welcomed. Introductions proved crucial pushes for those people intrigued by the idea of #LinkedInLocal but nervous about starting something in their area by themselves. Just introducing them to one or two more individuals in their location meant they had a team and felt more confident about jumping into planning an event. People were attracted to this new kind of event, one not focused on making money and sales.

The host community was a space to share ideas and therefore became something that not only attracted people to get involved but encouraged them to stay. Many hosts shared their successes and the lessons they'd learned. I shared a number of ideas that I had heard from others in the community. One idea was from an event in San Diego. At this event they decided to give people dots on arrival – the dots were representative of those who had shared videos on LinkedIn and those who were yet to create a video for the platform. During the event the more experienced creators were to team up with those who were yet to get started and make a short video at the event. This was a great example of #LinkedInLocal really helping others to feel more comfortable about engaging on LinkedIn, about supporting one another in creating content, and in turn enriching the online newsfeed to be more supportive and relevant to their own purpose. This is one of the many examples where #LinkedInLocal events enhanced the quality of content on the LinkedIn platform.

We were also keen for people in adjoining locations to open up lines of communication. For example, it was imperative that Miami and Fort Lauderdale hosts should know one another to cross-promote, minimise clashes and attend and support one another's events. These introductions were central to building the community of hosts. It also meant hosts with some experience – even if they'd organised only one event – could support new hosts as they emerged in the locations around them.

For me, personally, it wasn't just the offline events

that brought me a sense of belonging through face to face interaction but that sense of connection with like-minded adults that I'd missed in my world since starting my family. The community we were building online went beyond what LinkedIn had offered before. I had a real sense that collectively we were working towards the common goal of building a community and connecting people.

Whilst the host community enabled people to connect, the LinkedIn newsfeed still provided a lot of the 'noise' that enabled the community to grow. Hosts were able to share each other's posts, interacting and commenting on events in other areas in the public newsfeed – tagging in people they thought might be interested. This provided greater visibility of the #LinkedInLocal hashtag.

For the first few months of 2018 I was responsible for doing 90% of mentoring calls that were requested via the website. Erik, Alex and Swish continued mentoring enquiries via their own networks. At the time I was running four calls per week with six available spaces per call. A backlog of bookings for 30 days built up. People were joining calls at 2 a.m. local time just to get a slot. Every time we added a new call time it was fully booked in 24 hours. We couldn't have anticipated this level of demand from people wanting to get involved. The visits to the website continued to grow and we felt certain that we were losing significant leads with people who simply weren't able to get a slot on a call. We had no way for them to simply register their interest. We needed to expand our process further and we needed more people on board. In addition to the five #LinkedInLocal founders there are a number of people who impacted the movement. These people also contributed their time, ideas and experience, travelled at their own expense, and on so many occasions worked weekends and right through the night. They are deserving of a special mention and their voluntary hard work helped sprinkle magic across the globe.

Nicole Johnston, co-author of this book and a writer/ writing coach based in London, contributed her wonderful words for host and press communications and crafted many guidance and marketing documents, as well as story-gathering and storytelling for this book. Quddus Pourshafie, a lawyer, strategic advisor and problem solver based in Adelaide, Australia provided his 360 degree vision, and managed to marry what makes humans and business tick, and how we could make those two seemingly diverse aspects fit together. Gregory Caillol, an e-business strategist, based in Montpellier, France, initially pulled the French team together as a blueprint to help other groups pull together as countries, work together and support one another. Gregory continually provided advice, support and help with strategy and communications. Andrew Griffiths, a community builder and host in London and Vancouver, become a global cheerleader and shared his expertise to help the community to thrive. Javier de Torre Quevedo, a designer based in Spain, provided designs that became synonymous with the movement in the form of logos, graphics, illustrations brand guides, brochures and guidance documents. Dimple Patel based in Los Angeles, Nikola Agatonovic in Serbia, and Alex Leone in Washington DC, all contributed their product design and UX ('user experience') expertise for the website development and code development, and they dedicated a lot of their time in research.

In May 2018 we developed a proper host database which allowed individuals to register interest and we also introduced an informal pre-screening form. This not only helped people understand our values but allowed us to see if they had already attended #LinkedInLocal events and get an idea of their intentions. Curation of the community was still important for us but we did not use the form to filter out hosts or reject applications. All registrations were invited to attend calls to find out more information.

By this time the number of host community members was already over 400. This database, hosted by HubSpot and managed by Ryan and I, became central to keeping operations and events collaborative, especially in larger cities, as it allowed more people to share information with one another and allowed for the right introductions to be made after the website calls took place. New host applicants were registered automatically from the existing website and they were given access to the growing team of volunteers. As the community grew so did the number of questions. We developed more written guides, standardised branding, created fact sheets and event topic idea downloads for hosts to access via a resource centre. These resources were held in a growing, online, shared folder of documents.

The process was far from perfect, but our resources were next to nothing. We were a community of volunteers. The founders paid for the minimum of what was required – website, graphics, design, video conferencing – from their own pockets. We were reliant on people offering their services for free, on some occasions bartering, and on the support of those in the community with the time to spare to offer help. And there was a growing number of people from within the host community that wanted to volunteer their time to help serve the wider community. Some were direct in reaching out to help. Others we approached with requests and so many were delighted to help. All of these amazing people are gratefully mentioned in the acknowledgements of this book for their crucial contributions in building the community that #LinkedInLocal has become.

Looking back at the community we built I think what remains so interesting to me is that whilst it was never a requirement to go through our registration and call process to use the name, so many people *wanted* to. They were drawn to the idea of the movement – especially its values – and wanted to support it.

Asked in a survey in early 2018, 84% of hosts shared that their primary purpose for participating in #LinkedInLocal was 'to build community'. Many had been thinking about starting some kind of event already but for some reason hadn't taken the leap. It was the momentum of the movement that galvanised people. They felt connected to #LinkedInLocal and its values, and that's why they became involved and *stayed* involved. They wanted to be a part of something bigger than themselves, something not just under their own name. They wanted to be inspired.

Part Two: Stories From A Movement

Anna has taken you through how #LinkedInLocal got started, how she found her co-founders – or they found her – and how it became a much bigger community than any of us had expected.

As Anna observes – what started as a successful event for 15 people in Coffs Harbour, Australia – became something far bigger because so many people came forward to actively, vocally and virtually support it.

In this part we want to do two things. We want the people who took part – the #LinkedInLocal Family – to tell the story of how this movement impacted on them and their lives. In so far as we can, we have used their own words to tell their stories.

We've broken it into three sections to give you a taste of the feedback we got from people all over the globe:

The personal impact – the authentic connections and sense of belonging

The business and career impact – finding true purpose and activating leaders

The broader impact – on communities, charities, regions and even countries

After that, we'll take a look at the global context this took place in – what allowed this idea to take off in the way it did when so many similar ideas hadn't. What made a post from one woman who was missing face to face contact, turn into not only the most successful hashtag campaign on LinkedIn but – much more importantly – something that impacted on thousands of lives all over the world in such a positive and influential way? These are some of the things we've been asking ourselves and we wanted to share them here.

Our people, their words…

Authentic Connections and a Sense of Belonging

'You can feel the energy in the room. At our events we invite people to dance, let go and step out of their comfort zones. People don't want to leave. It's the buzz that is so addictive at #LinkedInLocal events and there's such a power there.'
Diana Nguyen, #LinkedInLocal
Melbourne, Australia

'I don't like networking events but the #LinkedInLocal events in Milwaukee are like a party with all the friends you haven't made yet.'
Mike Casavant, #LinkedInLocal
Milwaukee, USA

One of the goals of #LinkedInLocal was that people came to events as their authentic selves. It was a chance to get to know the real human beings behind the polished profiles. The events were intended to be inclusive, collaborative and to provide a space for everyone to belong. A lot of the stories people wanted to share were about the personal impact on their lives and these are the first accounts we're going to hear.

Erik Eklund is a co-founder of #LinkedInLocal.

> 'At our first event in the heart of Brussels, Belgium we are seated in the loft of a new restaurant. Menus are shared between the 15 participants – friends and strangers who all came because I'd invited them for an evening to get to know the real people beyond their LinkedIn connections' profiles. No one had any idea what this was about or what was to come, and neither did I. At that first event I had no clue this was part of the beginning of a journey that was going to cross more than ninety countries.'

As a co-founder of the movement, Erik was asked to attend and speak at many events around the world, one of which was in Kuala Lumpur, Malaysia. The invitation came from Alish Gholamali, who was planning an event there. Erik told us:

> 'Alish wrote me an uber excited invitation on LinkedIn and a month later I arrived in Kuala Lumpur wearing a sweater and jeans. I knew it would be warm, but it was 34 degrees and 98% humidity, and I had only one t-shirt with me.
>
> I still remember the look in Alish's eyes, "You only packed one t-shirt for Kuala Lumpur?"
>
> Kuala Lumpur was so far away but I had the friendliest of receptions. Strangers, including Aida Yeep, Carolina Correa and Alish, welcomed me with open arms and invited me into their homes to meet their families.
>
> I have so many more stories and I'm thankful for all of you who reminded the world what it is

to be human and that genuine relationships are easy to build when we choose to open up and get to know each other beyond our online profiles.'

□

Judi Fox started her career as a chemical engineer and got her master's degree in environmental management. In 2018 she was a single mum, working from home and running her own business in Richmond, Virginia, USA.

'I'd had a really, really tough four years so I'd been offline. In March 2018 I was running my own business and I got back online, looked at all of the platforms and saw what was happening on LinkedIn. I felt very encouraged by so many people in the community to make a video and express myself on LinkedIn. As I posted videos I started to connect with people like I never had before. As a result, I was feeling less alone. And I felt I had to go to #LinkedInLocal Dallas and meet people offline. My contact, Lila Smith, who I'd met on LinkedIn encouraged me to go.

So, I went to an event and it exploded my world. Meeting people, that I'd chatted to online, in person made me feel so connected. Now they feel like lifelong friends that will always have my back.

Now I am running the first #LinkedInLocal in Richmond and I'm really excited about it. None of this would be happening if I hadn't gone online, made that first video or turned up to a #LinkedInLocal Dallas event.

Thank you so, so, so much. It has completely changed the trajectory of my life.'

Gregory Caillol is an e-business strategist and is based in Montpellier, France. He is a both a host and host mentor and formed part of the small global team who supported the #LinkedInLocal co-founders.

'Throughout my career I've been to endless networking events and found them tiring. I would leave feeling drained and awful. I didn't have the experience or the title I was aiming for and I felt like a little guy from a village in the south of France where the ultimate ambition is to have a job to pay your rent. It was getting harder to start a conversation and keep it going.

I was in London for business and saw a post for a #LinkedInLocal London event. It was going to be held on the *Tattershall Castle* – a boat on the Thames river – on a very hot night in London. There were three other networking events being held there that night, so I spent the first part of the evening at the *wrong* event. It was the same as every other networking event I'd ever attended, and I didn't connect with anyone.

When I realised I was at the wrong event, I quickly found the one I was meant to be at. It was completely different, so much more than a regular networking event. The second I got there I felt comfortable – everyone was smiling and chatting. As people arrived, they were naturally drawn into conversations. It was relaxed and I could see people were *enjoying* meeting each other.

It didn't feel as though people were pretending or trying to be someone else – on the contrary –

the watch word was "authenticity". Everyone seemed to share the same values of respect and benevolence.

For the first time I had a sense of connecting with people, of belonging and having real, genuine and authentic social interactions. That night I met people who are still dear to my heart today.

Before #LinkedInLocal I'd spent a lot of time searching for people I could connect with and not finding them. It was like I was drinking at a fountain that couldn't quench my thirst.

I found my people through #LinkedInLocal and I kept finding them at event after event. It was a magnet for people like me. That first night was the night I fell in love with #LinkedInLocal.'

□

Melody Baron lives and works in Baltimore, USA and hosts #LinkedInLocal Baltimore along with Molly Browning.

'In Baltimore we like to listen, learn and experience. It's not just cocktails and business cards. We hosted the first event in January 2018, and we have been rockin' and rollin' every month ever since.

It's like a block party. Baltimore community members come together every month. They bring pieces of their businesses, their neighbourhoods and their personalities and provide us with an opportunity to explore our own city and the fantastic people in it.

I often work on autopilot. But when I'm hosting these events with Molly Browning, I feel like they are a part of who I'm supposed to be and what I'm supposed to do. The truth is it's who *we* are supposed to be, and what *we* are supposed to do. As humans, the very intimate act of connection is crucial to making the world go around.

I never thought these events would produce the beautiful outcomes I've witnessed. A local woman told me that she felt like she finally belonged. I had a transgender woman come to an event and, at long last, be recognised as a woman professionally. Another woman with a neurological brain disorder told me these events make her feel better.

This is a testament to the power of positivity and we most certainly can be more and do more when surrounded by the right people. We have several volunteers, all with day jobs, who do what they do because they believe in the movement.'

□

Ian McClure is an expert trainer and consultant in conflict, aggression and violence management. He lives in Warrington, UK.

'I attended #LinkedInLocal Warrington after more than four years away from networking events. I was already anxious but when the friend I was supposed to be going with cancelled at the last minute, it made me even more nervous. I wanted to be at my best, but I could feel a rise in my heart rate and a tinge of trepidation. People would probably say "It's not a big deal, Ian," and once upon a time I would've agreed with them but that was before my life took an unexpected turn.

I'd been working for years from six o'clock in the morning until nearly eleven o'clock every night dealing with a constant stream of complex and difficult cases in sexual exploitation – supporting vulnerable witnesses. I did a lot of networking back then and frankly I found it to be mercenary.

The upshot of those hours and that stress was that I collapsed in front of 30 headteachers at a conference. I had 36 counselling sessions but still ended up sitting in front of a psychiatrist refusing to take his advice and eventually I admitted myself to hospital voluntarily. I was afraid of the stigma. I insisted that I was just having a "cuff tupple of weeks." I spent four and a half months in a psychiatric facility.

Four years later and I found myself at the #LinkedInLocal event in Warrington, having overcome my nerves – and it was fantastic. The hosts – Kirsty James and Kate Jenkinson – should be proud of what they achieved. The panel and the other people in the room had great expertise. Since that first event I've continued to go along to events, and I know from the many stories I get to hear, that one of the most important things we can do is to learn to actively listen, without judgement and create safe spaces for people to be able to say they are struggling. It's important that the business community has discussions like the ones we've enjoyed about mental health, so we can look after each other effectively. I think the idea of #connectinghumans is amazing. Humanity and humility do go, absolutely, hand in hand.

I am so happy to say that I found myself in a very safe space and if this is how networks have grown in my absence then I'm very grateful.'

□

Brian Wallace is an infographics expert and – although he is originally from New York – he lives and works in Cincinnati, Ohio, USA.

'When #LinkedInLocal kicked off I really embraced it. I got to know all of the people behind the movement and then I became a type of mentor in my region. I kicked off a lot of #LinkedInLocal events and advised and connected people all over the country – in some cases across the world. I felt like my role mentoring and connecting people really helped cross pollinate and multiply the concept of taking your online network offline.

I can't stand a lot of in-person networking. It's a lot like speed dating. There's no context for meeting people. #LinkedInLocal events managed to connect the real people behind their profiles and offered valuable content at the events – experts giving great advice and information, without pitching. That's been a game changer for me.

These days I could roll up to any city in the world and catch up with someone I'm connected with at any time. I consider these people friends and extended family.

I'm one of 2,000 #LinkedInLive broadcasters so when I'm at an event I often go live – that way people on the internet can take part and ask questions as well.

The movement has been a game changer for me professionally and personally and I can't say enough great things about it.'

Nathan Yusuf lives in Romford, London, UK. He attended Alex Galviz and Andrew Griffith's #LinkedInLocal Youth events.

'Looking back a year or so ago, I think it would be fair to say that I wasn't the most confident of people. People would've described me as introverted. I avoided loud, social situations – partly because I never wanted to be in those situations – but the deeper reason was that I struggled to communicate effectively.

Fast forward to March 2019 and I was ready to change. I consider myself a proactive person when it comes to attending networking events and workshops so I couldn't turn down an invite to a #LinkedInLocal Youth event. Hosted by Alex and Andrew, the theme was how to communicate your story more effectively – to friends, family or prospective employers.

The guest speakers were Calvin Niles (communications coach) and Martin Brooks (impact coach). They provided me with the information I needed to build my confidence and enhance my communication skills.

Calvin recommended a ten-day "confidence boosting" regime. I initially found it daunting but soon I was completing the tasks with relative ease and less anxiety.

I had a graduation speech coming up at the London School of Economics for my study programme and it was the perfect opportunity for me to step outside my comfort zone. The speech was a success and I was nominated by the #LinkedInLocal Youth team to be the winner of a public speaking competition they had announced.

I feel a lot more comfortable with my ability to communicate and more relaxed about social situations. This is a change that will continue to benefit me in the future.'

□

Ewa Blonska is business advisor and lives and works in Wroclaw, Poland where she hosts events with Artur Trzebiński.

'We think that things occur because we plan them but so much can happen when time and space is available. The more goals and tasks we have in our calendars the less space there is for rare and remarkable things to happen. Additionally, we narrow our field of vision if we only connect with people from specific business environments and industries. It may be efficient only to meet people who are useful to us in our businesses or careers, but they won't always be meaningful connections. We expand our horizons if we meet people without the objective of monetising those relationships. This is especially true if we meet them outside the often formal business environment.

Artur and I created a space where people could connect, learn each other's life stories, to have time for rare and remarkable connections to happen and for them to go beyond business frameworks and broaden horizons.

Our aim was for people to leave feeling inspired, full of real emotions and an understanding that life isn't just about doing business. From the feedback we have had from participants, through surveys and what we've seen ourselves, we can see we've achieved that.'

□

Matt Gagnon, a life coach based in Austin, Texas, USA told us about a young man he met who we will call 'John' for the purposes of this book. These are Matt's words.

'I want to tell this story about John. He was probably one of the most special experiences for me because I met him at my first #LinkedInLocal. John was from Houston. He came to the Austin event and was very quiet. He was sitting in a corner, but you could see that he was trying to mingle a bit. He said he was out of work and living at home but that wasn't why he was there. John showed up because he wanted to learn how to be more extroverted. He was naturally an introvert, but he was trying to find the extrovert inside of him and learn to network. He felt like #LinkedInLocal was a safe space for him to work on that side of himself. That was super cool. I admired the hell out of him just for that. My level of respect grew even more when I saw him at the next Austin event because he was clearly going to see it through.'

□

Sagar and Mansi Amlani live and work in Hyderabad, India and together co-host #LinkedInLocal there.

'My story about #LinkedInLocal Hyderabad begins with the three core values which attracted me towards it – people are worth meeting; stories are worth sharing; and strive for collaboration not competition. It changed both my personal and professional life.

Professionally my networking had always been within my business community – the automotive industry – never with those outside of it. #LinkedInLocal opened up a whole new world because it was about connecting humans regardless of their profession. And it was about meeting the people behind their titles.

Personally #LinkedInLocal brought my wife and I together from our previously very separate routines when we started working together as co-hosts. At every event, meeting and activity, she was an equal participant to me, which definitely improved our time together. It brought a very sweet essence to our relationship where we could spend more time together and have more time to talk to each other.

I came to know so many new things about her in a professional context – in terms of her marketing, communication and PR skills. #LinkedInLocal gave me a new view on life, that it isn't only about a nine-to-five job, it's so much more than that. It gave me a reason to meet people, talk to them, grow and bring about change in people's lives. It also gave me strong friendships – true friends and real connections.'

Barbara Trepka runs #LinkedInLocal in the city of Olkusz, Poland.

'I first heard about #LinkedInLocal through a LinkedIn post by Bartek Ziemianski. Bartek wrote, "If you want to host a meeting in your city, let us know." I contacted him and he told me no one was organising these events in Olkusz and that I'd be welcome to start. I'd lived in Olkusz for two years and didn't know many people, but I did know that I wanted to do something good for my city.

I went to a #LinkedInLocal Cracow event and I was delighted. Two months later I organised the first #LinkedInLocal Olkusz event – 20 people turned up and it was great.

Organising these events has meant I'm more open to meeting new people and I've met so many. I've made new friendships and started new projects to benefit our local community. I am very happy I started hosting these events.'

□

Cathy Perez Stalgren is a content creator and runs her own business. She moved from the Philippines to Aarhus, Denmark in September 2017, after a stint in China.

'When I moved to Aarhus my confidence was low. I was jobless and knew very few people. I attended a couple of networking events, but none fulfilled my need to connect in a more genuine way. So, I decided to organise my own.

I heard about the #LinkedInLocal movement from a mention in one of Anna McAfee's posts and asked if there was one in Aarhus. There wasn't. Anna connected me with another woman who was interested and suggested we organise one together.

Around 40 people showed up to the first event – curious, friendly people who were open to new ideas. Many of them were trying to find their place in Aarhus – just like myself.

Moving to a new city is tough. I was trying to find my place, and organising #LinkedInLocal helped me to do that. It opened doors and opportunities that wouldn't have been possible if I hadn't done it.

Investing in real, human relationships is worth it. I haven't felt lonely in this city since I started hosting these events. There are always people to meet and many of my connections have grown into close friendships.'

□

Hordur Valsson is Danish. He works in holistic health in Aarhus and attends Cathy Perez Stalgren's #LinkedInLocal events there.

'I was born outside of the box and always had a different perspective on everything from those around me. After suffering from addiction, being subjected to aggressive behaviour in a horrible relationship, homelessness, mental illness and suicidal thoughts – amongst other things – I'd simply lost interest in doing anything.

I'd been planning a business to buy my way out of the country to give myself and my child the opportunity to live elsewhere once she turned eighteen but I'd lost momentum. That was when I found #LinkedInLocal Aarhus.

The theme at the first event I went to was *Disobedience and other forms of creativity* and it was filled with things I loved. I felt like the speakers were describing me! Even better was that, for the first time in years, I was socialising with inspiring and interesting people.

Since the event I've made a supercharged return to my plans. I've started creating content and I've become a speaker myself. Too many of us don't get the encouragement we need to move forward with what we love. I wake up every day, knowing I'm making it happen and that my goal will become reality.

Had it not been for #LinkedInLocal I'd probably still be complaining about that reckless psychiatrist from 2014 or anything else to keep myself in eternal lockdown.

Instead I'm putting my reflections into LinkedIn articles which will eventually be included in my book. The working title is *Your Parents Effed You Up & It's Your Job To Fix It*. I was born as a rebel. I'm finally living like one and I intend to go out making noise.'

□

Brian Schulman is a digital marketing expert based in San Diego, USA where he hosts #LinkedInLocal events.

'I loved the idea of taking online relationships offline and into the real world. Being able to meet so many amazing people, and then bring them together in ways they had never done before changed everything for me.

We used Zoom to livestream from our very first #LinkedInLocal with two other locations around the world – with Anna in Coffs Harbour, Australia and an event in Baltimore, with Sonny Tannan.

That was our very first event. It was an incredible day and a magical experience to have together. We felt as though we were better together – we felt like family. #LinkedInLocal was what brought us all together to be able to truly impact the world.

Our events were about lifting one another up and bringing people together – to show people they aren't alone. I think that's huge because it helped people feel like they were a part of something.

#LinkedInLocal provided a place for us all to be able to share our experiences, to bring our hearts together and to be more creative as a community.

We provided folks with a safe space, let them know they had a voice, a story that matters and – more than that – their voice and story can positively affect the lives of other people in ways they never thought were possible.

Coming together through conversation and getting over our fears has made such an enormous impact on my life and on so many other's lives.'

☐

Brooke works as a consultant and attends events in Baltimore City. She is transgender and has asked that we don't publish her surname as she works in a conservative industry environment where her transgender status is not currently public knowledge.

'I can't be me all the time – 24/7. Personally, I have no problem with it. When I'm on the road for work I post pictures on Facebook all the time – of me – being me. I love it – it's great. The best thing I ever did was to open up a Facebook account and check the box for female. However, I work in a very conservative industry and they don't know. I'm frightened that if they did it would be the end of my career.

When my LinkedIn contact, Allison, invited me to come down a #LinkedInLocal event in Baltimore, I decided to go. But I told her, "I need to tell you I'm not coming down as the person you know on LinkedIn". She said to go for it. I was nervous as hell. But when I got there, I had no problem – none whatsoever. I've been back three times since then and I've never had an issue.

I love Baltimore City. It's special because it made a big difference to me. That I can connect my personal and professional life and be me has impacted hugely.'

☐

Samson Cakpo hails from Cotonou, Benin and specialises in branding and social media. He was introduced to #LinkedInLocal by Raegan Fatouros and Anna McAfee. He was mentored and supported by Gregory Caillol in France. He introduced the #LinkedInLocal concept in Benin and, alongside local co-hosts in Mali, Senegal and the Ivory Coast, he has spread the benefits of #LinkedInLocal and the idea of #connectinghumans through French speaking Africa.

'I joined the #LinkedInLocal community after I heard about the first events organised by Anna McAfee in Coffs Harbour, and Gregory Caillol in France. I knew immediately I should be part of this great community with values in perfect alignment with my own – collaboration, diversity, authenticity and respect for each other. I had a call with Raegan Fatouros – then another with Anna afterwards.

Since then have co-hosted events in Cotonou (Benin), Abidjan (Cote D'Ivoire), Bamako (Mali) and Dakar (Senegal) with locals in those locations.

These #LinkedInLocal events changed my life. I've met some extraordinary people from my LinkedIn network that I never imagined I would meet. I have made meaningful connections that have led to business opportunities. I am very honoured to have made this journey. I've grown mentally and emotionally and I'm proud to have made a big start with something great.'

□

Aminata Koumare got involved in #LinkedInLocal when she co-hosted her first event with Samson Cakpo in Bamako, Mali.

Aminata says she has always been very sociable, but through these events she has met even more people. She credits hosting these events with a boost in her confidence and says that they have enhanced her sense of self-respect. More than that, she says that it increased her understanding and appreciation of others. Aminata said, 'Thanks to those who have trusted me and have chosen me. Thanks to them I have found my way.'

□

Lila Smith is based in Dallas, Texas, USA. Today she is a public speaker and consults on communications and branding.

'When I retired from acting I kind of lost my community. Being alone was a new feeling and I didn't like it. I felt unimportant and overlooked so I went on LinkedIn to renew connections with people.

It was June 1, 2017 that I began connecting on LinkedIn. It was a new way of "communing" for me – digitally, professionally – and it gave me something of a sense of belonging. But I still didn't know the humans beyond their LinkedIn profiles. They were also based all over the world and sometimes I just wanted to have cup of coffee, a hug or dance it out with them in person.

I connected with Rachel West Palombo, a marketing director, through Adam Karpiak, vice president of a recruitment firm. Rachel and I clicked.

She told me about #LinkedInLocal events. She'd spoken with Anna and Erik and asked me if I would co-host #LinkedInLocal in New York City events with her. Of course I agreed that I would.

It happened fast. Co-hosting the events I started recognising my gifts in community building, making connections and putting together programmes. I went to events, speaking gigs and travelled to other #LinkedInLocal events. Soon I was a global host mentor, running onboarding calls and mentoring new hosts from around the world, advocating for active inclusion.

I started seeing myself the way others did – as a leader. So, I leaned into my community – yes, it was a community, both a local and a global community – and knew I wouldn't fall far if I decided to take a big leap. I leapt into working for myself as a professional speaker and trainer. A month later I moved to Dallas. I had realised that a good chunk of "my people" seemed to be in Dallas, and they were mostly entrepreneurs.

Because of my connections through the global community I made the move to Dallas with eleven hours' notice. I arrived with interviews set up, clients to work with and people to eat every meal with if I wanted to. Dallas was my "new local".

These events – they're not just networking events. They're community makers. My life was forever changed because of #LinkedInLocal and I know I'm not the only one. I will say that when people get together with the sole purpose of truly *seeing* each other, chances are someone who really, really needs it will *feel seen*.'

□

Michael Lalonde lives and works in Ottawa, Canada.

'I wasn't always doing as well as I am now. My mother and father were both addicts and my mother lied to me and herself about that. I grew up believing it would be impossible for me to ever do well. I constantly lived in poverty and knew nothing else. My mother left, taking a large chunk of my savings for college without my permission but I managed to get through school, get a bunch of loans, and reinvent myself.

I had a chip on my shoulder and thought the world owed me. I got my first career role at Coca-Cola and thought I was going to do great things. When our entire division was gutted, I was devastated and bounced from job to job. I've had a myriad of jobs throughout my career. I've learned a lot along the way, including how to be humble and that, as humans, we have very little control over the big stuff. But what *does* matter and *can* make a difference, is connecting with others.

This is the crux of how I became involved in #LinkedInLocal. I'd been inspired to try and turn failure into success by Michaela Alexis, a digital marketing expert and one of the speakers at an event. I also met Scott Berty, a marketing and social media guru and host mentor, and Joel Hansen, business development manager, at events. They encouraged me to see that I could make an impact too.

I started to help organise the events and, when Scott decided to take a huge opportunity and move to Toronto, he felt more than happy to hand the reins over to me. Ever since then I have been bringing in more people and trying to pass that good fortune along to them. It is with those connections and meaningful conversations that anyone can go from hopelessness to happiness. Raising others up is the greatest reward I think I've ever got.'

□

Jaime Cohen is based in Denver, Colorado, USA and is a speaker and communications coach.

I've been a comedian, a competitive salsa dancer, a public speaker and a performer as well as an all-round fun person to hang out with. A few years ago, my mom was diagnosed with a really rare form of breast cancer and all that changed. The original prognosis was two weeks, but we got twenty months with her. But, when she passed away, I felt totally helpless. At the time, I was working for a company that didn't treat me very well. So, I retreated into my shell. I went from being independent and an entertainer to a shadow of myself. I developed severe social anxiety and PTSD. Whenever I went out, I would count down the hours until I could go home.

I saw increased engagement on LinkedIn around this time and when I checked it out, I saw people having real conversations and posting about something called #LinkedInLocal. They described their events as taking your online connections offline. I've been a proponent of that my entire digital life. I was really excited about the idea.

I've performed in front of thousands of people in my life, but I don't think I've ever been more nervous than I was when I co-hosted Chicago's inaugural #LinkedInLocal event and spoke in front of the 130 people who attended. It was the worst performance of my life, but I can confidently say that I'm proud of it because I had the support of my co-hosts and the #LinkedInLocal community. It gave me so much confidence that I decided to try again. At the second event, I moderated a panel instead. It was more like a conversation between friends.

  I now have friends all over the world and I've been doing a ton of travelling. Meeting your online friends in person for the first time is a crazy feeling, it's indescribable.

  For the first time in five years, I feel more like myself and that wouldn't have happened without #LinkedInLocal.'

□

Surabhi Srivastava lives and works in Lucknow, India, as a trainer and consultant.

'I was, professionally, in a dark space having had a setback in my job. I felt like I was going nowhere. I'd lived in UK for over a decade and then moved to a small town in India.

Lucknow is famous for its food and heritage but in terms of professional and corporate development it needs to grow. A friend posted about #LinkedInLocal Lucknow. I went along and left feeling rejuvenated and happy.

When the host position for #LinkedInLocal in Lucknow became available I jumped at the chance to organise the events. My first event was a sell out!

It was the best thing that had happened to me in a long time but then I got the biggest news of all. Fourteen years after my son was born, I discovered I was pregnant again! I hosted another two events before the Christmas #LinkedInLocal event and then my daughter was born in January 2019. So many of the #LinkedInLocal members came to shower their blessings on her. I found my tribe – my support system. I've since started my own business, and it's started growing gradually. It's been a challenge, but the members have stood by me.

I've had accolades, challenges and even friendships come out of #LinkedInLocal. People recognise me and come and say thanks for bringing such great events to the city. The appetite for them just keeps growing and so does my confidence.

Many friendships started, people left their unhappy jobs to pursue their entrepreneurial dreams and have had loads of support from the community. When someone in our group had an accident – members even gave blood. I get messages from near and far as, although Lucknow is a small city, those who have left look back and see their hometown being part of this global thing and they love it. I honestly cannot describe the positive things these events bring.'

□

Jacob Wierzbicki lives in Dubuque, Iowa, USA and spends his days building brand recognition through content creation.

'#LinkedInLocal changed my life. Seriously, that's not just a clickbait, eye-catching sentence. Let me explain... I'm weird. I'm an introvert. I believe in hard work and leaving the planet a better place than when I arrived. It's important that I challenge myself. Understanding these motivations is significant as there are millions of people who can relate to this mentality but there are millions more who don't. At that time I was surrounded by those who didn't. I started to believe *I* needed to change in order to "be normal" until I found LinkedIn and the #LinkedInLocal movement.

I came across this social movement when I was asked to speak about personal branding in Austin, Texas. I'd been told I speak well but I'd never spoken on that topic or to a group of people who I assumed knew as much as I did. I mustered the courage to go. What I found was beautiful. A group of people – from anywhere and everywhere who were weird and introspective.

A little over 100 people showed up. My talk lasted about 30 minutes and I had an absolute blast. Folks came up afterwards and asked questions and before I knew it was ten o'clock at night.

On the way back to my hotel – I realised how emotionally high I was. I thought about how many people had said, "Thank you, that changed my perspective." I realised I live my life wanting to make a difference and hoping that I can make a small impact on the lives of others. It's a real buzz to know that you've opened somebody's mind to a different way of thinking.'

I love speaking and sharing my story. The emotional high that comes from knowing you have truly made a difference gives the greatest sense of fulfilment and satisfaction.'

□

Patrick Ward, a marketing director and host of #LinkedInLocal in LA, USA, told us why he considers #LinkedInLocal events to be very different to standard networking events.

'In LA we set out to create an environment in which people want to keep coming back. When people come to events, they're seeing their friends and I like to think of it like a family reunion. I've had the chance to get to know other people on screen, now I get to see them in person and speak directly to them.

Even when you're speaking to someone in video format it's not quite the same. There is an energy to being in someone's physical presence – when you're standing right in front of somebody – and I think that's really what #LinkedinLocal creates. Conversations can begin online and start at that base level and then offline we obviously talk about business, but we also talk about life, motivations and careers – all these other aspects. I think that has been what has been key to our success in LA.

When I go to standard networking events and everyone's trying to pitch, trying to sell. You listen to a bunch of elevator pitches; you collect a bunch of business cards and that's it. But you don't get excited to come back every single time. And that's, I think, the unique thing that #LinkedInLocal events have captured versus what everyone hates about networking.

The demand for these events is based on people responding to the values and principles around the events being community driven rather than profit driven. People have had business opportunities from these events but it's not the driving purpose of them.

  #LinkedInLocal acts as a bridge between online and offline and in a very positive way that creates even deeper relationships. At the end of the day, social media should be social. And this is what I think #LinkedInLocal does in a way that I haven't seen any other platform really do.'

□

Agnieszka Wnuk lives in Poznan, Poland where she now works in the same company as Bartek Ziemianski, who introduced her to #LinkedInLocal. She co-hosts events with Beata Ratajczak.

'In June 2018 my friend, Beata Ratajczak, and I both read a post about #LinkedInLocal by Bartek Ziemianski.

Although we're both shy, we decided to host the first #LinkedInLocal together in our city Poznan, Poland. We have a good relationship and work well together.

I host these events because I feel they help people to really talk to each other. I love it!

As a result of hosting #LinkedInLocal events, I feel stronger in myself and I have more confidence. I know that people have a good time and that we create a happy atmosphere at our events.

These meetings inspired me to start my own business as a LinkedIn consultant and strategist and I now work in the same team as Bartek Ziemianski.

I'm convinced, now that I am part of the #LinkedInLocal community, that nothing is impossible!'

□

Kassy Pajarillo-Braganza lives and works in Manila, the Philippines. She co-hosts events with Joey Gomez, Raymond Braganza and Lysa Sanchez.

'It gave a jump-start to so many things and all of it was beautiful… it helped thousands believe in themselves more and be advocates of lifelong learning, collaboration and friendship.'

□

#LinkedInLocal created lifelong friendships, bolstered waning confidence, soothed social anxiety, gave people the opportunity to be their authentic selves and essentially changed lives all over the world. The movement brought local communities together but also made the world feel slightly smaller. Any city or town with a #LinkedInLocal event felt a more welcoming space. Accountant, Linda Bolton would agree. Her #LinkedInLocal journey started with an impromptu journey to Hong Kong to a Future of Work themed event. Her next stop was to one of Jillian and Jane's events in Sydney and last but definitely not least she met Jessica Diaz Nunez in Peru. #LinkedInLocal was not the only thing Linda and Jessica had in common – over lunch at an art gallery they discovered they shared the same profession. Linda came back to Sydney inspired and set up a #LinkedInLocal group in North Sydney.

Matt Gagnon told us, 'I could turn up to almost any city I can think of right now and know that I have a couch to sleep on.'

Finding True Purpose and Activating Leaders

'#LinkedInLocal has created really impactful experiences where I have learned to get out there and collaborate in a community where everybody helps each other bring their thoughts and their projects forward.'
Nina Polo Marcellier, #LinkedInLocal Noumea, New Caledonia

'Bringing the LinkedIn Local event to Albany, NY was the best move I made in 2018! The highly attended events and actively engaged participants brought my spirit back to life after a personal and professional loss during that time. It's an event that changed it all for me. #LinkedInLocal gave me a platform to not only reach those I wasn't reaching before, but it gave my connections and community an open and safe place to learn, share, and grow from people they'd never had the chance to meet!'
Miranda VonFricken, #LinkedInLocal Albany, USA

It's a simple fact of life that most of us want to work with people we like and can relate to, and so we tend to give contracts, jobs and form partnerships with those we feel we can collaborate well with. So, whilst #LinkedInLocal events were strictly pitch-free, it was inevitable that work partnerships would form. If you create a space for like-minded people to come together and connect in an authentic way with people who share common values and principles – extraordinary working relationships can be formed.

These are just a few of those who wrote to us about their experiences of #LinkedInLocal impacting on their careers. Some found their dream jobs and some even found their true purpose.

□

Scott Berty lives in Toronto, Canada and works with Swish Goswami at Trufan, a social intelligence platform.

Scott has long since forgotten who hooked him up with Anna McAfee, but Swish Goswami and Joel Hansen, a business development manager based in Vancouver, are the likely culprits. After an initial chat with Anna he was sold on the values that the events aimed to embody and offered to help.

He co-hosted an event in Seattle in February 2018 and posted about it on LinkedIn. Since then he's co-hosted and helped out with several events in Ottawa and Chicago.

What makes Scott a special member of the #LinkedInLocal Family is that he – quite accidentally – became a crucial source of information for the #LinkedinLocal community. He became a go-to individual for anyone wanting help setting up their first events. Scott shared his expertise and experience with whoever asked for it before we'd even recognised the need for host mentors. He was, in a sense, a host mentor before we'd even coined the name.

Scott told us how much he enjoyed being around in the early days as the movement grew. He feels that it impacted on his ability to connect with people. In 2018 Scott lived in three different cities in as many months. Despite that upheaval, Scott regularly got on calls to prospective hosts offering his advice and experience and he still helps new hosts out wherever he can.

He credits the first #LinkedInLocal Ottawa event he co-hosted with Joel Hansen, along with some help from Nika Moeini, an alumni relations manager based in Toronto, with catapulting him to where he is now. There were some amazing speakers at that first event – including Michaela Alexis, a LinkedIn trainer, and Swish Goswami.

Swish and Scott had already connected online before they met at the event. Scott knew that Swish was a start-up entrepreneur and they'd discussed the possibility of working together. This event was the start of a friendship and a working relationship for both Scott and Swish. Two years later Swish and Scott started working together on *Trufan*, a platform which helps brands and influencers discover, activate and reward their key followers. '#LinkedInLocal,' Scott told us, 'helped shape the life I now know today.'

☐

Andrew Griffiths lives and works in London, UK as a project manager. He has been a host and a host mentor.

'My #LinkedInLocal journey began when I attended my first #LinkedInLocal London event in October 2017, hosted by Alex Galviz, who I now count amongst my closest friends. I've hosted #LinkedInLocal events and attended them in three countries since then including an event at Science World in Vancouver's iconic waterfront organised by Mohammad Asadi Lari and Yonden Sherpa, and an event in Los Angeles organised by Joel Hansen, Nate Kara and Natalie Riso where we got to hang out with the LA Clippers and take in a basketball match. But I had no idea how a few simple conversations at that first event in London would escalate.

At that event in London, Alex and I discovered that we shared a passion for developing up and coming young leaders. After our conversation, Alex started to organise a collaboration with Pearson College London to deliver our vision for #LinkedInLocal Youth. The topics we wanted to cover weren't usually addressed within either academia or work. For example, we wanted to explore networking both online and offline, leveraging LinkedIn, wellbeing at work, telling your story in an impactful way and selling yourself.

Ticket prices supported a charity called The Brokerage who help young people from disadvantaged backgrounds enter education and gain work opportunities in the city. We invested in a livestreaming camera to broadcast the events, enabling more young people to participate around the world.

We witnessed a huge transformation in the young attendees coming to the #LinkedInLocal Youth events. It was hugely rewarding and acted as a fantastic platform for numerous people to share their wisdom with young people in an incredibly impactful way.'

Andrew's life and career have been significantly impacted through the time and effort he has invested in #LinkedInLocal but more than that, it's the impact that he and Alex have had in transforming the lives and opportunities of young people that forms his #LinkedInLocal legacy.

□

In many cases #LinkedInLocal led attendees to job opportunities but it also helped people access new communities upon moving to a new location. **Raegan Fatouros** and **Khatija Qureshi** created #LinkedInLocal New To Canada in Toronto. Their objective was to help migrants in their new country with a local community of friends, contacts and, potentially, new roles. The following two stories are from people who attended their events as newcomers to Canada.

Gurinderjit Singh Bajwa arrived in Canada in August 2018. At Raegan and Khatija's event Gurinderjit heard about a Speed Mentoring event run by one of #LinkedInLocal's supporters BMO (Bank of Montreal), where he met some of their senior managers. When a role as Financial Services Manager was advertised Gurinderjit was able to use his new network to guide him through the process. He was successful and started in January 2019. Gurinderjit said, 'I would like to thank Khatija and Raegan for all of the help and guidance in settling in Canada as a newcomer.'

Anushree Mandal attended her first event in May 2018. She connected with Khatija after the event who told her about a human resources contract that had recently become available. Anushree was successful and this become her first role in Canada. Anushree said, 'I am always so comfortable speaking to you and asking for any help needed. Thank you for being so approachable.'

Priya Dhawan lives and works in Pune, India, where she is a brand specialist. She is a host mentor and was responsible for supporting many other hosts in India to launch in their communities.

'#LinkedInLocal helped me find my "why" and since then my career has changed 360 degrees – from a jobseeker to an entrepreneur and founder and director of a private limited company where I work as a brand strategist and collaborations expert. I used to suffer from stage fright and now have my first invite to be a guest speaker and address business owners and corporate executives. I moved from a world of office politics and toxic colleagues, to a world of endless love, respect, acceptance and encouragement from the local community of 1,500+ online strangers who have become offline friends and collaborators. I "found" myself and understand my strengths, potential, capabilities and horizons have gone global.'

□

Germain Louie moved to Santa Monica, California, USA in June 2019 for a role with NetSuite.

'Going into my final year of university, I didn't know what my "true calling" would be. I'd placed a lot of importance on my first full-time career opportunity playing a pivotal role in my entire career.

My involvement in #LinkedInLocal Orange County, California, meant that I had the opportunity to expand my network more than tenfold. Whenever I travel to a city, I never feel alone because there are community leaders around the globe who have this shared experience and would welcome me. #LinkedInLocal has allowed me to continue to lead with a servant's heart.

#LinkedInLocal gave me multiple opportunities to pave the way in my career to work for or collaborate with some of the largest companies and industry experts, including in my current role with NetSuite. From being stuck in a daze in trying to understand where to go next – I can now see that everything happens for a reason.'

□

Brian Almeida lives in Toronto, Canada where he works as an entrepreneur.

'The #LinkedInLocal movement changed my life in many different ways. Whether it was introducing me to great friends, or the incredible sense of community – I felt just being a part of it was amazing. I will forever be grateful for it. I was first introduced to the idea by my friend Erik Eklund who, like many of the founders, is someone I'd never actually met in person. This is one of the many great things about this movement, it introduced a new way to connect and build community. At the time I was struggling with who I was and where I wanted to go in life, and Erik said I should connect with Anna McAfee, the originator of #LinkedInLocal.

I had no idea that this journey would lead me down a path to public speaking. #LinkedInLocal not only inspired me to start doing this but provided multiple opportunities for me to speak.

All I know is I have never felt so connected and so full of inspiration. In this day and age it is so easy to get caught up in the digital world and build a ton of online connections. This movement defined what it meant to bring your online connections offline, to connect as humans again, to build friendships and relationships that will last for years to come.'

□

Godwin Chan is based in Mississauga, Ontario, Canada and spends his days as an assistant event manager.

'When Swish Goswami posted about #LinkedInLocal I asked him about holding these events in Montreal. It was Anna McAfee who responded and connected me with John Marrett who was also interested in running the events there.

John and I have such different backgrounds – he's a Montreal native and his family is from Jamaica. I'm second generation Chinese Canadian, born in Toronto. In many ways we're worlds apart but we got along very well because of the shared passion that we had for creating communities and bringing online to offline.

Together we set up #LinkedInLocal Montreal.

We connected over coffee and he helped me get my bearings in Montreal.

At our first event we had about 20 to 30 people attending, with a couple of guest speakers.

I co-hosted three #LinkedInLocal Montreal events before I moved back to Toronto. John and his team are still organising great events there.

Before #LinkedInLocal I'd been set on becoming a doctor. I'd completed a science degree and met all of the requirements to apply to medical school in Canada. I was so close but realised that my passion was now for connecting people, organising #LinkedInLocal events and building communities rather than spending time in a laboratory.

My interest increased in business, networking, entrepreneurship and connecting with people. I joined Bobby Umar's #LinkedInLocal Toronto team. It's a way for me to really get to know other people and to help them. I've started my own business as an events manager and I'm writing my first book. This has been a transformational experience for me.'

☐

Nicole Jovecevic lives and works in Chicago, USA as a career development specialist.

'#LinkedInLocal came at a critical time in my transition from association management into what I truly wanted to do – career coaching. I didn't know how I was going to make the leap, so I simply started creating workbooks and coaching people on the side for free.

I got tossed into the #LinkedInLocal Chicago pool thanks to Scott Berty, one of our host mentors, who connected me with people here locally. It was truly remarkable to be a part of it.

Almost everyone at the event was an entrepreneur or someone who was transitioning into business and, more importantly, they were willing to help and provide feedback. I didn't know *any* entrepreneurs or innovators, so it was a completely new world, and one that I felt welcome in.

It gave me the courage to start posting on LinkedIn – something which hadn't occurred to me before – and, once I'd taken the leap, attending the events pushed me to continue making videos and content.

It was this that gave me the courage and the belief in myself to make the bigger leap and since then I've been working in my dream job as a career coach at a non-profit organisation. And I work with people on the side through my own coaching business. I know my life will evolve from here too, but #LinkedInLocal gave me the momentum and the community to propel me into my mission and execute my vision.

Plus, I got to pay it forward by coaching some attendees for free and helping them land new jobs! It's a continuously giving community and a local/global partnership focused on bringing people together.'

□

Tamar Hela lives and works in Shanghai, China as chief operating officer for a company offering LinkedIn marketing expertise. She is also a published author.

'I got an offer to move from the USA to China in 2016. I barely knew Shanghai but now it's one of my favourite cities. I'd created a LinkedIn profile years before but I just considered it to be a great platform for potential job hunting and no more. In my second year living in Shanghai someone told me that LinkedIn was evolving so I decided to check it out. It added to my network – and I loved that – but something was missing – that in-person, human touch. Enter #LinkedInLocal. There was no chapter in Shanghai at that moment so I decided to jump on board. Growing my network is a vital part of thriving while living and working abroad and this seemed to be the ideal opportunity.

In August 2018, #LinkedInLocal Shanghai was officially launched on a Thursday night… with a typhoon right on our heels. I didn't know what to expect for our opening night with such extreme weather – after all a typhoon isn't just a little drizzle. Imagine my surprise and delight when about 120 people turned up! Rooms were packed to capacity and everyone was in high spirits and enjoying networking despite the blanket of sub-tropic humidity.

My life in Shanghai has changed since that first event. I'm connected to so many valuable people in various industries and I know that help of all kinds is just a text away. I've attracted new clients and projects, as well as created partnerships with venues like the American Chamber of Commerce in Shanghai. With a population of 26 million people this city needs events that can connect professionals on a more intimate level. I'm seen as an influencer in China because of my role hosting #LinkedInLocal Shanghai.'

□

Zain Gaziani lives and works in New York City, USA in his dream job as community manager for Team GaryVee.

In 2017, Zain Gaziani was objectively a success as an HR business partner for Amazon at a very young age. He knew he was incredibly fortunate to be working for them but, at the same time, he started to realise that he wasn't in the right place for him. He left Amazon and, in a post on LinkedIn, he thanked them for the opportunity. On his first day searching for a new role he noticed a post about a #LinkedInLocal event in Canada and decided to go.

It's not unusual for attendees and hosts to go to #LinkedInLocal events in other countries but it's not usually their very first event. Zain drove to Canada and met George Khalife, Swish Goswami and Michaela Alexis who all encouraged him to post about his job search journey on LinkedIn.

Encouraged and inspired, Zain started to share more content on the site and engage more with other users. After listening to Gary Vaynerchuk (Gary Vee), an author, entrepreneur, speaker, podcaster and internet personality, Zain joined Gary Vee's Facebook groups and offered help and advice to the community. Zain later applied to be a moderator for Gary Vee's Facebook community and was successful. Zain realised that his passion was in community management.

Zain eventually met Gary at one of his official events in Dallas and bravely asked him for a job as his community manager in a Q&A session in front of the room full of attendees. Gary offered him a job in New York. Zain jumped at the chance, made the move and took the job.

Zain was later invited to be the keynote speaker in Vancouver at Mohammad Asadi Lari, Andrew Griffiths and Yonden Sherpa's event.

□

Quddus Pourshafie, a lawyer and problem solver, co-hosts #LinkedInLocal Adelaide, Australia and also became part of the small global team supporting the co-founders to steer the movement.

Quddus told us he was looking for a way to open up dialogue and community in a networking capacity that cut deeper than the typically superficial networking events. He yearned for deeper connection and #LinkedInLocal was the first movement of its kind he found that opened him up to new people in an organic and real way. Hosting events helped him to come out of his shell and made him more comfortable in his own journey of entrepreneurship. By being able to interact with other professionals in a human way, he was able to also discover how valuable he could be regardless of titles and roles. #LinkedInLocal ultimately helped increase exposure to some bigger ideas and thinkers and supported his idea to develop a business and pathway to look into the future of the legal profession, rather than pursuing the status quo of that industry.

☐

Naveen Prakash hosts #LinkedInLocal in Chennai, India.

'I'd seen posts about #LinkedInLocal events and how communities were being built around the world. When I saw that these events were being organised by just normal people with regular jobs, I decided I would host an event in Chennai, India.

It was important to me to build a meaningful community without pitching, selling and meaningless discussions. I knew these events were putting people together to share knowledge, getting to know other professionals and specifically empowering women and students.

The help and support provided by the #LinkedInLocal community, especially from Anna McAfee and Priya Dhawan, was invaluable. I knew from the beginning that it wouldn't fail.

Personally, I've become an extremely confident person thanks to hosting #LinkedInLocal events. I had a fear of public speaking and have now spoken in front of more than 5,000 people in just a few months – this is a great personal achievement. Professionally, I've made amazing business contacts and my credibility as a community leader has been established.'

□

Nelson Bonil hosts #LinkedInLocal in Lyon, France.

'I heard about #LinkedInLocal events through my friend Gregory Caillol, a host mentor in Montpellier, France. He convinced me to get out of my comfort zone and host these events. This happened just as I graduated and was looking for my first job.

When I started this new adventure, I had no idea how much it could help me launch my career. Meeting networkers and creating a very engaged local community was a great challenge especially in France's second biggest city.

I have to admit that the first speeches I made were hard but organising, promoting and engaging Lyon networkers to come to the events was a fabulous experience. I've met hundreds of people in Lyon but also from very far away and I've built great relationships.

The comments I receive after every event are always supportive and have been a great source of motivation. After a few months, thanks to visibility the #LinkedInLocal Lyon events get, I got a job in digital marketing and communications. I'm glad to say I keep hearing stories of people who have found internships, started collaborations, made huge leaps in their professional career or launched projects because of the help given by those they met at these events. That feels really satisfying.

I am less introverted now and I have amazing connections. I feel proud of this community and the "ready to help" mindset we all have.'

Aashad Mason hosted #LinkedInLocal events in Rochester, New York, USA.

'I got involved with #LinkedInLocal because I'd heard about the events in Washington D.C and Atlanta, Georgia. I called a connection I had, Ally Willinsky, who was already involved with #LinkedInLocal in Atlanta. She explained the vision and the purpose in less than sixty seconds and said, "Mason, you're a go getter, start one in your hometown. Set up a call with Anna McAfee."

That day I booked a place on one of the online onboarding calls that Anna and her host mentors offered to people who wanted to become #LinkedInLocal hosts. When the day of the call came, I was nervous, excited and curious. Anna was calm and confident and answered all of our questions.

After the call, I got to work, called my business mentor and convinced them to help. I recruited eight people to help me with the first event in less than seven days. In 2018, we hosted four events. At the first event, over 60 people showed up and we had a blast. I met more than 125 local people that year.

My #LinkedInLocal experience helped me land two awesome jobs and has given me the confidence and the skill set to take up leadership roles.

I am still young and grew up in the inner city. Before #LinkedInLocal I had no degree or credentials and I felt insecure about not having that college education. But after my experience with #LinkedInLocal, I had a different type of life experience to back me up. To this day I'm seen as an event expert because of the success of #LinkedInLocal.'

□

Michelle Minnikin co-hosts #LinkedInLocal in Newcastle, UK with **James Eves**.

'James and I met through hosting #LinkedInLocal events and soon discovered we had a lot of common interests. James had always wanted to start a podcast and the universe had conspired to introduce me to a chap who owned a podcast studio. Our weekly podcast *Inspiration North* launched in January 2019. Now we run events, volunteer to run Action for Happiness courses and are using the podcasts as a foundation to write a book and develop services to help people find their purpose. Our mission is to fly the flag for the North East of England, create a movement for people to raise their aspirations, take action and create more fulfilling lives for themselves. We use research and analysis to show how people have found their passions and in doing so, we have a lot of fun. It's a passion project. It means we speak to and learn from inspirational people and help spread their messages.

We have found our purpose. We've become business partners – best friends – and in each other have found the person we are meant to be with. We are excited about what the future holds.'

Jillian Bullock co-hosts #LinkedInLocal in Sydney with **Jane Jackson**, and was the host mentor for the Australasia region. She held her first solo event in November 2017 but it wasn't long before she met Jane who came on board as co-host. Meeting Jane and running the #LinkedInLocal events has made a huge difference to both of their lives. There is a lot of synergy between them and that has led to another successful collaboration – they launched their successful *LinkedIn with Jack and Jill* Podcast in November 2019. They cover LinkedIn branding basics for business building and career management explaining how to really leverage LinkedIn to expand people's professional network and lead generation.

□

These events didn't set out to provide business partnerships and collaborations – the primary purpose, unlike other networking events wasn't to make business happen. But by creating a space where people could connect as their authentic selves – beyond a job title, beyond a LinkedIn profile – we created the opportunities for like-minded souls to come together to make magic happen – and they did.

Creating Lasting Impact

'Through human connection, we have settled differences, learnt from the stories of others who are different from us, and seen the world from a different perspective. Time spent with great minds in other sectors is always rejuvenating and this is why #LinkedInLocal has improved healthy relationships between professionals.'
Ojo Oladimeji, #LinkedInLocal Ibadan, Nigeria

'We are a passionate group of professionals from the City of Joy, united around the belief that with authenticity, respect and collaboration, we can unlock the door to successful,
meaningful, value-driven, ethical, joyous and sustainable living.'
Debasish Biswas, #LinkedInLocal Kolkata, India

We didn't envisage this chapter when we first planned this book. We knew that #LinkedInLocal events had raised money for charities throughout the world and we wanted to celebrate that. However, in the feedback we received after Anna's request for stories for this book, we were astounded at just how profound the reach has been. The funds raised for various charities were one achievement, but the impact went beyond that. Communities, charities and, even countries, saw shifts and impacts that we could not have foreseen, all as a result of #LinkedInLocal.

In this chapter we share just some of the many stories we were told, and we can only guess at just how many more we haven't heard about yet.

These are a few examples of the money raised at #LinkedInLocal events for charities all over the world. Sometimes contributions were large, others were small, but all were significant. The #LinkedInLocal Family has contributed a substantial amount to charities and so many hosts have worked tirelessly to raise these funds to make an impact in their local areas.

Not all events collected money, many events were run free for attendees. However, where hosts were collecting money to cover costs, they were encouraged to use any surplus money to support local charities in order to remain not-for-profit, to ensure consistency with the founding values of the movement.

□

#buy100bales campaign and #LinkedInLocal Sydney, Australia

Jillian Bullock and Jane Jackson – co-hosts of #LinkedInLocal in Sydney – held a panel event in November 2018 with the primary purpose of raising funds to support New South Wales' drought-stricken farmers. Droughts are not usual in Australia but that year was one of the worst on record and it was having a significant impact on farming communities.

Australia had a broader #buyabale campaign running with the objective of buying bales of hay to give to farmers who had no feed left for their cattle. Farmers were having to slaughter their stock as they could no longer afford to feed them. To support this campaign and, in particular, New South Wales farmers, Jillian and Jane kicked off their fundraiser, #buy100bales, for their November 2018 panel event.

Whilst using social media to raise the profile of the upcoming event, Jillian and Jane managed to capture the attention of celebrities and members of the Australian Parliament. The MP for Gilmore, Ann Sudmalis, who is from a farming family, reposted the event telling Jillian and Jane that her family were having to slaughter ten cows a day at the height of the drought. The speaker at the event, Warwick Merry (past President of Public Speakers Australia), donated his time for free as his family are dairy farmers, so it was a cause close to his heart.

In a clever strategy and using social media, Jillian and Jane encouraged those who couldn't attend the event to contribute to the #buy100bales campaign as well. So, several other members of the #LinkedInLocal community around the world made donations to the cause. Shay Rowbottom, from Miami, and Zach Scriven, from California, came all the way from the US to support the event.

It was a huge success and exceeded their objective, raising enough for 111 bales – and demonstrated to New South Wales' farmers that many supported them in a show of solidarity.

□

Blue Dragon
Project Renew
#LinkedInLocal Ho Chi Minh, Vietnam

Vietnam was the 91st country to hold a #LinkedInLocal event. Before she moved to Vietnam, My Holland had lived in Australia and had attended #LinkedInLocal events in Sydney and Anna's events in Coffs Harbour. Upon arriving in Vietnam, My felt that Ho Chi Minh was the right place to kick off Vietnam's first #LinkedInLocal. She was keen to raise the profiles of critical social issues in Vietnam and also raise funds for charities. She charged for her events and the profits were then handed on to local charities.

Their first event was for Blue Dragon – a charity which supports impoverished Vietnamese children in danger of being trafficked to China for sex slavery or to work in sweat shops.

Blue Dragon's donor relationship manager, Ms Hoa, flew in from Hanoi to be the guest at the event. In her address, she revealed that she had given up a high-profile career as an investment banker to work for the charity and help preserve the safety of these children. She felt she had found her purpose. Ms Hoa later thanked the event attendees saying, 'Your donation was used to provide vocational training for five survivors of human trafficking. Learning a trade has enabled them to find a stable job and stand on their own feet. Minh (not her real name) is one of the five young women who reaped the rewards of educational support and vocational training that you have provided. Minh was born into a poor family with six children. As an older sister, she had to drop out of school when she was in grade four to help her parents with farming. At the age of nineteen she was tricked into being trafficked. Even after she was rescued, her nightmare wasn't over because of the stigma from her community. She cried day and night, feeling desperate about her life and future. Blue Dragon kept in touch with her to provide psychological support and career advice. Finally, Minh decided that it would be best for her to move to Hanoi and enrol in vocational training. The first period was not easy, because Minh wasn't fluent in the mainstream Vietnamese language. However, she was determined to overcome her challenges and, within six months, she graduated from her training course in cooking. After graduating Minh found a job as kitchen staff at a high-end Japanese restaurant in Hanoi. Minh's life has changed for the better. The support from My and #LinkedInLocal helped five trafficking survivors build themselves a better future.'

At their second event My and her attendees raised money for Project Renew (Restoring the Environment and Neutralizing the Effects of the War), a charity that works to remove and make safe remaining American UXO bombs (unexploded ordnance) in Vietnam. According to the Ministry of Labor, Invalids and Social Affairs, unexploded bombs have been responsible for more than 100,000 injuries and fatalities since 1975, rendering many of the survivors permanently disabled. My's event raised $200 (USD) and the money was earmarked by Project Renew for victim assistance, disability support for those injured by these devices and reinforcing UXO safety messages in young people.

Adarana Orphanage
#LinkedInLocal Hyderabad, India

Husband and wife team, Sagar and Mansi Amlani harnessed their #LinkedInLocal events in Hyderabad to raise money for local causes. They ticketed the events and donated the proceeds to support a local orphanage, Adarana, which cares for 40 children. Sagar and Mansi would raise between 2,500 and 5,000 rupees at each event for the orphanage. Some of the contributions they've made have been used to buy curtains for the girls' bedrooms, throw birthday parties and buy gifts and treats for the children. Their efforts have also contributed to ensuring that the orphanage's stock of stationery, foods, grains and vegetables are set for up to a year. Recently they have organised for schoolteachers to read the children stories and a happiness coach to teach mindfulness to them. Their efforts have made a profound difference to the most vulnerable in their local community.

□

Living Classrooms Foundation
#LinkedInLocal Baltimore, United States

Baltimore's #LinkedInLocal events, hosted by Melody Baron and Molly Browning, raised $30,000 over the course of 2018 and 2019 through ticket proceeds and sponsorship fees.

The money raised was donated to the Living Classrooms Foundation, based at the Masonville Cove Environmental Education Centre in south Baltimore. Once a small settlement, Masonville Cove became an industrial area in the 1950s and eventually a dumping ground. Work began to reclaim the land for the community and nature in 2007 and in 2009 the education centre, based in a state of the art, green building was opened. The area is now home to 230 species of bird including Baltimore's only pair of nesting bald eagles and is an astounding area of natural beauty, free for residents to visit and enjoy. Living Classrooms is a not-for-profit organisation that aims to disrupt the cycle of poverty and violence within Baltimore communities by helping young people build life skills through small-group, hands-on education in health and wellness.

□

The Autism Community in Action
#LinkedInLocal Orange County, United States

In Orange County, Lucy Beaudette and Germain Louie held their first #LinkedInLocal event in September 2018. The proceeds from ticket sales were given to The Autism Community in Action. The event was a sell-out. Several #LinkedInLocal Family members from other cities, including Matt Gagnon and Brian Schulman, came along to show their support.

After that event some attendees came on board to help Lucy and Germain run future events, including Vasudha Srinivasan, Unati Patel, Diana Trinh, Jon Salas and Asuza Tarn.

This team went on to organise another fundraising #LinkedInLocal event in May 2019, for Working Wardrobes. The organisation is run by volunteers with the objective of transforming lives through the dignity of work. They aim to empower clients with both job skills and confidence to find meaningful employment. Their career success institute holds workshops, training opportunities and other work readiness services to men, women, young adults, veterans and seniors. Alongside these other services they also provide second hand, business attire for clients for interviews. They receive 500,000 annual clothing donations to fund their client programs and they have helped 105,000 clients since 1990.

Lucy says, 'I can't thank my co-hosts enough for everything they do, the time they spend away from their loved ones and their own activities to build a community with me.'

Breast Cancer Haven
#LinkedInLocal Portsmouth, United Kingdom

One thing #LinkedInLocal Portsmouth co-hosts Ian Gribble and Carl Hewitt were sure about was that they wanted their events to benefit local charities. For each of their events they chose a local charity to receive any money raised above costs and to gain from raising their profiles in the local community. For their first event they chose Breast Cancer Haven, an organisation that provides a comprehensive programme for women and men either during or after breast cancer treatment. The Haven offers a tailored package of emotional, physical and practical support and for costs to be covered it works out at £1,000 per person. The funds raised at the event paid for the entire programme for one breast cancer patient. The Guildhall Trust was another of the beneficiaries from #LinkedInLocal events in Portsmouth, which aims to become one of the UK's leading organisations in enhancing cultural enrichment within the local community.

□

The Brain Tumour Trust
South West Children's Hospice
Empire Fighting Chance
Tree Aid
#LinkedInLocal Bristol, United Kingdom

Host mentor, Greg Cooper, donated ticket prices for his #LinkedInLocal events in Bristol to local charities. Greg approached local venues and asked them to provide space for the events. Each one of Greg's #LinkedInLocal events raised around £650 for a charity.

Greg's objective was to support a different local charity at each event and he specifically looked for those that were less well known – who would not only benefit from the donation but also from raising awareness of their cause.

Greg's events in Bristol raised funds for several charities including The Brain Tumour Trust which supports patients, families and friends of those diagnosed with a brain tumour.

The South West Children's Hospice were also a chosen charity and they provide palliative, respite, end of life and bereavement care for life-limited and terminally ill children and their families from the South West England region. Another worthy cause was Empire Fighting Chance, established to help young people from deprived backgrounds using non-contact boxing and personal support to inspire them to reach their potential. Bristol-based, Tree Aid also received a boost from the events. Tree Aid is a charity that was set up to help people in the drylands

of Africa to grow and protect trees which are critical
to their income, environment and survival.

□

OzHarvest
#LinkedInLocal Canberra, Australia

Kat Krikorian and her #LinkedInLocal team in Canberra, Australia, donated all of the money made through ticket sales to their events to raise funds for a national cause, OzHarvest. OzHarvest collects quality excess food from commercial outlets and transports it to around 1,300 organisations who support disadvantaged people all over Australia.

Through the money their tickets raised #LinkedInLocal Canberra donated more than 22,500 meals to Canberrans in need of a feed.

Kat says that they chose OzHarvest because it meant that the funds stayed local and helped people in their own neighbourhoods, many of whom had no idea where their next meal was going to come from. She told us that they regularly invited up to four local charities to set up stalls at their events. They actively encouraged their attendees to consider how they could contribute to their local communities through supporting these organisations and in doing so they raised the profile of some of Canberra's smaller charities. They also supported start-ups whose work assisted Canberra communities.

□

As well as raising a lot of money for charity the #LinkedInLocal movement also worked to address some of the global issues that affect us all. These are some of the stories we received of events making a real social impact in their communities.

Mental Health in the Workplace
#LinkedInLocal London, United Kingdom

Mental health in the workplace quickly became a popular theme for #LinkedInLocal events across the world.

Alex Galviz hosted an event in London in 2018 with a focus on the topic. A huge range of people attended – mental health professionals, therapists, HR directors and people who have themselves suffered from mental health issues in the workplace. Alex says:

'It was the sort of conversation that needed to be had but that would've been difficult to have in a sales-related or corporate environment where many would have found it uncomfortable to express themselves honestly and openly. The simple goal of the event was to bring people together to share stories and to provide a safe space to talk about the challenges they and others faced. Having gone through my own struggles I wanted to create and provide something that I couldn't find when I needed it.'

She later posted about this event and others around the world contacted her to ask how they could create the same safe space for these conversations in their communities.

Modern Slavery
#LinkedInLocal Derby, United Kingdom

Lesley Brown, host of #LinkedInLocal in Derby, UK, brought Paul Callum, director of the Slave Free Alliance, to talk to attendees at an event. Paul's organisation works with companies and businesses to raise awareness about modern slavery and then assists them in ensuring that their supply and distribution chains are not unwittingly reliant on the slave trade. In September 2019 Derby police arrested thirteen people in relation to the largest modern slavery operation in Derbyshire – the gang involved were jailed for 33 years. This local case helped Paul bring the message home to the local business people at this event. Awareness is key to ensuring modern slavery is identified and that local companies are aware of the need to ensure their supply chain is slavery free.

□

Global official satellite event for gender equality – Women Deliver (2019) #LinkedInLocal Vancouver, Canada

In the summer of 2018, Karin Tischler, Director of Research and Development at the Daimon Institute for the Highly Gifted, was touring in Europe visiting other #LinkedInLocal hosts. She met hosts, Maximilian Niedermüller (Salzburg) Karen van Hout and Omuzua Ameze Isiramen (Luxembourg), Patricia Wiesner-Dumont and Sarah Santacroce (Lausanne) and Martina Haas (Berlin). Karin shared her plans to contribute to running a gender equality conference with Martina who used her extensive social media network to link Karin to some gender equality organisations.

Karin held her first #LinkedInLocal event in Vancouver in January 2019 and although it was a small event she met Rahul Moodbidri, who had just moved from Montreal. He agreed to co-host with Karin and their events started to get more attention and more attendees. Karin approached 'Women Deliver' who organise the largest gender equality conference in the world, held every three years. She asked if her next #LinkedInLocal event in May 2019 could be a satellite event for their conference. She was delighted when they agreed, and their Canadian Mobilisation team sponsored their satellite event. Invited by Karin, Humphrey Nabimanya, founder of Reach a Hand in Uganda and a speaker at the wider conference, sent a video welcome message for Karin and Rahul's event. Karin told us that she and Rahul were particularly pleased to have raised awareness of the Women Deliver conference and its mission in Vancouver.

Diversity event after New Zealand terrorist shootings in mosques
#LinkedInLocal Hamilton, New Zealand

On March 15th, 2019, two mosques in Christchurch, New Zealand were the scene of a violent attack by a lone gunman. Fifty people lost their lives and the tragedy resonated around the world. It was the deadliest terrorist attack on New Zealand soil in modern history. Questions were raised about the influence of populism and violent racist rhetoric. It was a time for reflection, not just for New Zealand but for the whole world.

In the north of the country, host of #LinkedInLocal in Hamilton, Daniel Hopper, held an event in the wake of the dreadful news with the theme of diversity. Already an embedded value within the #LinkedInLocal movement, it was particularly powerful and poignant in light of the attacks. One of Daniel's Muslim colleagues, Ahmed Saleh, brought his children to the event and spoke about the events in Christchurch from his perspective.

The event's key message was 'We won't be divided'. With one quarter of New Zealanders having been born overseas, the goal was to take a stand against the racism that had fuelled the attack and to reinforce the relevance and importance of diversity. Daniel felt this was an important moment for Hamilton to make its support for the Muslim community clear. At the event attendees wrote messages of support to Christchurch and the local Muslim community showing solidarity. These were printed on a banner by one of the attendees, Ken

Choe, and the banner was shared with hosts in Rotorua, Auckland and Christchurch for their #LinkedInLocal events. This event and the sharing of the banner by other #LinkedInLocal events throughout New Zealand brought local communities together at a critical time to demonstrate and reinforce that everyone in these communities is valued and must be allowed to feel safe.

□

Sowing the seeds in countries and regions

It would be remiss not to talk about those who went the extra mile to bring these events to those in their communities and further. We had host mentors who facilitated and supported hosts all over the world to provide a space for everyone to belong in their communities as listed in the acknowledgements.

On top of that a few dedicated souls went out of their way to ensure that those in their regions had the opportunity to attend #LinkedInLocal events in their countries. This has not only impacted the lives of the individuals hosting and attending events but the communities they live and work in.

Here are some notable examples.

French-speaking Africa

With support from Gregory Caillol, Samson Cakpo took the #LinkedInLocal message to many French-speaking countries in Africa. He ensured that, in every country, he engaged, supported and mentored local hosts to ensure the sustainability of the events. Samson co-hosted with Adjaratou Lawani (Benin & Cote D'Ivoire), Marie-Nadège Oyoua, Marie-louise Soundele, Assetou Kone (Cote D'Ivoire), Aminata Koumaré (Mali), and Rodrigue Adjiguidi, Sabine Sombie and Bocar Laurent Sy (Senegal). They have improved the opportunities for so many individuals and communities in French-speaking Africa. We have received so much feedback from those local hosts thanking Samson for his help and support getting started.

Just one example of the impact the people driving these events are having in their local communities is that of Virginie Mounanga, and the #LinkedInLocal team in Gabon. They began hosting #LinkedInLocal events in Libreville and have since been invited by the Minister of Communication and Digital Economy to train the country's national congressmen on how to represent their country on LinkedIn. Certainly, the opportunities in that one country alone for Virginie and her team, and Gabon, are very likely to be positively impacted thanks to the dedication, commitment and support of Gregory, Samson and the local hosts in making this space available for their local communities.

□

Latin America

Evelyn Andrade hosts #LinkedInLocal events in Fort Lauderdale with Kelly Merbler. She is originally from Panama, had lived in Columbia and has an extensive network in Latin America. She started posting about her events and putting contacts from Latin America in touch with Anna. Anna eventually asked her to be a host mentor for the region.

A friend of Evelyn's from college, Jaime A Cardozo, saw the #LinkedInLocal posts on her feed and immediately fell in love with the concept. He started events in the main cities of Columbia – Bogota, Cali and Metamign. Evelyn also contacted and mentored people to host events in Panama, Argentina, Dominican Republic, Jamaica and Mexico.

The Caribbean

Pauline Joseph hosts #LinkedInLocal events in Trinidad and Tobago and Barbados. When she spoke to us for this book, she was looking at the possibility of events in Guyana and Jamaica so that people across the whole region could benefit from them.

Pauline said, 'In the Caribbean we suffer from an inferiority complex. We often believe someone with an accent must know more than we do. We're using the #LinkedInLocal network to showcase the amazing talent we have across the Caribbean and we're slowly changing that perception.'

☐

Poland

Bartek Ziemanski also spread the word about the value of #LinkedInLocal and mentored hosts across Poland to bring these events to their local communities.

That #LinkedInLocal events could potentially bring not only opportunities and confidence to individuals but communities and regions is more than anyone could have hoped for.

Why This? Why Now? And Why Us?

'It's time to connect. To take our online connections offline, face-to-face. To meet real people, in the real world. Meet the locals, old friends, and make some new. Talk life. Beyond job titles and business cards. Just us, humans, because each of us has a story to tell. It's time to inspire each other. To think about what our common future could be like. How can we make things happen? Together!'
Bea Pole Bokor, #LinkedInLocal Nelson, New Zealand

'We built a community, we danced, sang and found our real-life friends at #LinkedInLocal Singapore'
MS Suchi, #LinkedInLocal Singapore

#LinkedInLocal was such a simple idea that it came as no surprise that Anna McAfee wasn't the first person to think of it or the first person to coin the name. In 2018, the co-founders became aware of a group in Austin, Texas that had been running for some time under the banner 'LinkedIn Local'. A standalone group, they had been running events in their local area well before Anna made her first post to locals in Coffs Harbour. Bringing online communities together was not a revolutionary idea. Swish recalls that he was inspired by YouTube broadcasters who organised gatherings of fans in locations they were visiting. There was something in the water at that moment in 2017 that meant that conditions were perfect for the start of something global. In this chapter we're going to look at the global environment, both culturally and in terms of technology, that provided fertile ground for a movement that would spread through over 90 countries, firing up the passions of hundreds of people and affecting the lives of thousands.

□

The Digital Media Revolution

We've all experienced at least some part of the digital media revolution. There are very few of us whose lives haven't been impacted significantly by the advent of computers, the internet, email and smartphones.

A significant feature of this revolution is the massive scale adoption and daily usage of social media platforms, disrupting the way we'd done things for decades. Here is a potted history.

According to Saqib Shah's[1] article about the history of social networking the first steps included Bulletin Board System (BBS) where people could download games and files, AOL, and CompuServe.

By the 1990s the internet was growing fast; Yahoo was set up; Amazon started selling books; and personal computers (PCs) were starting to become more common in people's homes.

First versions of social networks included Classmates.com which in 2016 still had 57 million registered users. There was no facility for profiles, but you could search for classmates online. In 2002 Friendster launched, a website which its own CEO, Jonathan Abrams, described as 'a dating site that wasn't about dating'.

It was the year 2003 that saw LinkedIn start up as a network for professionals. Today LinkedIn has 660 million users and 303 million active monthly users. Myspace kicked off the same year.

In 2004 a Harvard-only online network started up, called Facebook. It was made available to the broader public in 2006. Facebook went from 1 million registered users in 2004 to 2.4 billion active monthly users in June 2019.

YouTube was launched in February 2005 and by May 2019 it had reached 2 billion monthly logged on viewers worldwide.

Twitter launched in March 2006 and by 2019 it had 330 million monthly active users.

□

Increased connections and accessibility

One of the advantages to the rise in accessibility of digital media has been an increased capacity to connect with our online networks, both personally and professionally. It's easier than ever to do business on a global scale. Digital technologies have meant increased access for many who may previously have been excluded from participating in the labour market – people with disabilities, those with caring responsibilities or without access to transport are now more able to take part in remote employment or run their own businesses.

There has been a proportionate increase in flexible working arrangements with information accessible from any working space in many roles, in a vast array of industries worldwide. Research conducted by Pew Research Centre[2] in the US in 2014 showed that five years ago 21% of those surveyed worked outside of their office either every day or almost every day and 50% worked somewhere other than their office occasionally. This was made possible because of the availability of digital technology – many are able to rely on the internet, mobile phones and computers to be able to work in places other than their offices. The 2020 Coronavirus pandemic has made this resilience and shift to remote work more important and widely prevalent.

The capacity to communicate with colleagues has become a major benefit of some social media platforms and digital technologies. Some companies have even adapted existing social media platforms to encourage collaboration amongst their employees.

Productivity

Alongside the increase in the flexibility of work there are claims productivity has increased up to 84%[3] over the past four decades because of digital technologies. That figure is astounding but what makes it credible is that these technologies have made it much easier, quicker and more effective to communicate with our colleagues in real time and information from all over the world is literally at our fingertips. We have all benefitted from being able to simply type searches into a search engine and have journals, academic works and press articles available to us in seconds. It makes sense that these two factors would impact on people's productivity.

□

Changing workplaces

Many of these factors have contributed to a change in the way work gets done. The workplace arrangements of previous generations are no longer as available as they were. The days of spending an entire career working for the same company is unlikely to be an option for current and future generations. Even individuals who stay on the same career track are likely to require at least one change of company.

Many of the jobs in the labour market now didn't exist two decades ago. Perhaps more surprising is that 60% of future jobs[4] available will be completely new to those of us in the workforce today, indicating further significant change is expected.

□

The gig economy and portfolio careers

Two terms unfamiliar to us before the global financial crisis of 2007-2008 are 'gig economy' and 'portfolio careers'. Out of the straitened financial climate of the crisis many who had previously enjoyed permanent roles found themselves making a living by 'gigging' – picking up short-term contracts, freelance opportunities, and part-time roles to make-up their income. Although the 'gig economy' was born out of necessity there have proven to be a lot of advantages both for individuals and organisations. Companies are more easily able to outsource work to freelancers and contractors, where they are unable to justify the permanent cost of an employee. For individuals it has meant more flexibility and choice about the work they take on.

Out of this came what has become known as a 'portfolio career'. It refers to people who have more than one role to ensure they can maintain an adequate, liveable income level.

In the case of a portfolio career a worker receives income from several roles – part-time, temporary, freelance or contract. Some work in full-time roles but also have what is becoming increasingly known as a 'side hustle'.

This in turn has resulted in the rise of personal brands. With many on the market able to provide a range of services in their fields, having a recognisable identity in the market has become a necessity to stand out amongst competitors. This has coincided with available technology and social media platforms to make promoting and marketing your personal brand more accessible.

☐

Community building and civic participation

Community building has become easier thanks to the increased availability of digital technology. Previously, people relied on face to face interactions, telephone calls, email, or other written communications – often making the process slow and laborious. Social media platforms have provided an instant, real time way of connecting with like-minded people all over the globe whatever their shared interests or goals. Charities and community groups have been able to build support, promote their work and raise funds online.

Social media has definitely been a force for increasing civic participation. 'Digital media is helping to amplify the response to humanitarian crises and to support those afflicted.'[5] One example was the Arab Spring of 2011-12 where social media was used to disseminate information, provide a centralised resource for protestors and organisers, and to raise the profile of the issue to the wider world. There are reports of refugees fleeing war-torn regions using Facebook and Google Maps to identify safer routes and to keep out of the hands of people traffickers.

□

This is the global context we think that allowed #LinkedInLocal to thrive and impact on the lives and communities of those involved. The massive increase in take up of digital technologies and social media platforms has led to a huge increase in online connections and networks.

However, whilst it became easier to grow networks and do business from behind your computer screen there were some side effects. Perhaps the most significant of all was a human connection gap created by digital interactions replacing physical ones. It was this sense of disconnect that created a need for something like #LinkedInLocal. The advantages of digital technology were plentiful but reduced many of us to contact mainly through a screen. All of the features that united us in online communities and freed us up as a global workforce have also caused many to feel isolated at the same time.

More flexible and remote working arrangements, while very convenient and inclusive, have led to an increase in social isolation. Anna was a perfect example – she didn't lack connections or an impressive network – she was lacking face to face interaction. So, while our ability to build a global network online has increased it has meant a consequent human connection gap resulting in an increase in loneliness and social isolation

Humans are social beings who need interaction with other people. Some neuroscientists claim that our need to connect with other humans is as important as our need for water and food. Human contact is a need that stems from when humans literally needed each other for survival. The 'pack' or community needed each other for safety, for sufficient food and water, and for care. This need has adapted over time. Most of us, very fortunately, no longer need others for literal survival in the way early hunter-gatherer communities once did but the need for those connections are still as critical to humans' well-being as they ever were.

Humans, like other animals, suffer when their connections are under threat. This might not fit cultural notions of individualism but 'the facts are the facts' according to neuroscientist Matthew Lieberman[6]. He makes clear that any trends towards 'self' and other more modern concepts don't reduce our need for connection as it is a critical human need. Lieberman is not alone in his claim that connection between human beings is critical to health and well-being. A lack of it can, therefore, be significant to human happiness.

We know, when we experience difficulties in our lives, having a network around us is crucial to the way we cope with these challenges. There are reports that social connections can boost our immune systems, while a lack of them can lead to depression, loneliness, and anxiety.

Loneliness and social isolation have become significant contributors to depression. They 'feed' each other. Loneliness can exacerbate depression and anxiety, and depression can cause people to retreat, to isolate themselves further. Sadly, as people become lonelier, they can tend to move towards the periphery of their social groups, adding to their sense of isolation. There are even experts who suggest that loneliness can be contagious – that it has the capacity to spread through groups of people.

According to the UN, a significant proportion of the world's population have mental and psychosocial disabilities. One in four people worldwide will experience mental health difficulties at some point in their life. One million people take their own lives every year, and suicide is the third highest cause of death amongst 15 to 19 year olds. If that doesn't focus us on the importance of this issue, then this quote from the UN will: 'Depression is ranked third in the global burden of disease and is projected to rank first in 2030.'[7]

The good news is that, according to a Harvard study[8], people with strong, social networks are not only generally happy but healthy. The connections we have on a daily basis don't have to be deep, even 'passing' interactions, including online, can have a positive impact. Those social contacts release oxytocin – a happy hormone –which reduces feelings of fear and anxiety

We consider this human connection gap – an unfortunate 'side-effect' of the growth in usage of digital technology – to have been a key factor in the success of #LinkedInLocal globally. It was no surprise that when Anna, Swish, Erik, and Alex posted about the first #LinkedInLocal events, people began asking questions and became engaged with the idea themselves. Anna had no idea that globally there were hundreds of thousands of people who were missing face to face interaction and by posting that day she was tapping into an appetite for something like this. #LinkedInLocal was something that appealed widely, and people came forward in their hundreds to bring it to their part of the world.

Community is an often-misused word. People use it widely and assume it means a following that might quantify your social media 'reach', but a following is a metric – not a community. Community means something different – it refers to a group of people who come together for a common cause. It is not something contrived or created for marketing purposes by clever companies or by brilliant social media managers. #LinkedInLocal is a community, in the true sense of the word.

More than a community, #LinkedInLocal became a global movement or what our dictionary defines as 'a group of diffusely organised people or organisations striving toward a common goal relating to human society or social change, or the organised activities of such a group'. Movements are largely driven by the grassroots, by the people on the 'frontline'. This has been a significant factor in the growth of #LinkedInLocal. It came out of a desire for more interaction by one isolated human being in Coffs Harbour – mirrored over and over by people with a similar need all over the world. And that appetite is still there. It's sufficiently there to keep busy people showing up in Coffs Harbour, Sydney, Hyderabad, Los Angeles, Dakar, Shanghai and over 650 other cities across the world. People don't just 'create a movement' – it doesn't just *happen*. People will not give their time for something that doesn't resonate with them at a deep level, especially when there is no monetary or other direct reward. Networking events take place all over the world every day. What we have come to realise is that the reason #LinkedInLocal was different was because it *wasn't* a networking event, or at least not as we've come to understand them. As Swish Goswami observed, 'If this is just another networking event, why do people just keep coming?'

So, what was it about #LinkedInLocal events that worked at this time? One of the recurring answers to this question from the #LinkedInLocal Family was that the values and principles established by the co-founders and their small support team were communicated clearly and adhered to. The values were what made the movement stand out.

Swish goes on to say, 'It all stemmed from the way Anna set it up, with hosts helping each other out with a strong sense of community. It started from the top – Anna, Alex, Ryan, Erik, and I – we put out a very positive message which made people feel included and want to consider becoming hosts. That only happened because of the culture we created for these events – inclusive from the beginning. If you came to #LinkedInLocal you never felt like an outsider.' The values of authenticity, inclusivity, respect, and no competition provided a safe space for people to bring their true selves.

Ryan Troll, another of our co-founders based in the United States, notes that, 'We groom our LinkedIn profiles meticulously, engineering what we imagine ourselves to be… but our most memorable conversations are probably fairly authentic rather than feeling artificial and engineered.'

Networking events are often seen as a place for the

extroverted and confident to thrive. At #LinkedInLocal events, space was provided for everyone regardless of their employment status, role, or seniority – all were welcome. There was a richness in the experience because of that. Many self-identified introverts felt comfortable attending #LinkedInLocal events and some even chose to host them in their communities. Introverts are certainly not islands and their well-being relies on other people for contact, support, and friendship as much as anyone else. Jacob Wierzbicki, attended events in Austin and Madison, in the USA and co-hosted Dubuque events. Jacob describes himself as 'weird and introspective'. He told us he'd thought that to get by he would need to change in order to 'be normal' but he found 'weird, introspective people' just like him at #LinkedInLocal events 'and it was beautiful.'

Another reason that the #LinkedInLocal environment made so many feel at home is the subjects and issues many events chose to address. Rather than the standard sales and business-related conversations that many find superficial at networking events, #LinkedInLocal communities sought to explore larger and more weighty issues. Small talk and sales pitching were replaced by authentic conversations about real community issues.

John Austin-Brooks, who hosts events in Bath, United Kingdom, told us, 'The concept of not being sales focused appealed to me. Getting to know a person just as themselves is a major part of any relationship – transactional or otherwise.' His counterpart, Greg Cooper, host of #LinkedInLocal in Bristol, United Kingdom, agrees, 'Some people are nervous about networking so being able to meet in a non-promotional environment is more inviting.'

So many people quoted in this book have expressed the view that social media is *social*, and therefore about people. It is not about technology. Technology is the vehicle – the tool we use to achieve our objectives, to connect people. Tim Berners-Lee, creator of the World Wide Web, said that he hoped *'the Net would be used to cross barriers and connect cultures.'*[9] We think that #LinkedInLocal is an excellent example of exactly that.

#LinkedInLocal happened because of a moment of serendipity – pieces of magic came together in a global context of increasing usage of digital technology and increased online connections that was inadvertently fuelling social isolation and loneliness. It was simply the right time, the right place, and the right people. The world was ready for #LinkedInLocal. We lit a fire for those who wanted to communicate offline as well as online, and in a more human way. We sparked a movement for people who wanted to connect with a whole person and not just their professional profile.

Part Three: Legacy

Passion, Problems and
a Corporate Conundrum

'#LinkedInLocal was a genius whisper campaign which created a sizzling hype to the platform. It was where younger contributors could give the platform a second chance at becoming the next best social platform instead of an online resume holder. It was brilliant.'
Chantel Soumis, #LinkedInLocal Madison, USA

'Hosting #LinkedInLocal events with my students at The Hague University of Applied Sciences has been excellent experience for all of us to develop various lifelong learning skills. From first hearing about the concept in class as a branding case study, to planning and promoting events, welcoming guests and expanding our networks – it's also been a lot of fun.'
Renée Veldman-Tentori, #LinkedInLocal The Hague, The Netherlands

'Mummy, I need you to put down your phone!' I heard my four-year-old daughter yell at me. And I smarted because I knew that this wasn't during 'Mummy's work time' this was during time I should have been spending with her and her two-year-old brother.

For 18 months I had managed and grown the #LinkedInLocal community on what I'd *planned* on being a part-time basis. But the project was demanding. Everyday community management, meeting host demands, growing resources, producing content that reiterated our values and – probably the most time consuming – answering endless questions from new joiners. I was, personally, being crushed by the sheer demands on my time that this very hungry community was taking up.

Each of the co-founders, including myself, were all running businesses and managing families and, alongside our normal lives, trying to steer the movement that had grown beyond all expectations. I was the lead community manager for our host community, and I was still running some of the mentoring calls from the website bookings and co-ordinating the availability of the other host mentors. I have always been a good listener and good at connecting people – it was a role that came naturally to me and one I loved. I wasn't being paid for the work, and yet I found myself often more driven to help hosts create authentic connections and to build communities, than I was in the everyday LinkedIn training I was offering through my own business. I enjoyed meeting both online and offline, globally and locally the many incredible human beings that were getting involved. The sense of connection it created for me was the thing I had been missing back in 2017. I realised that many people underestimate the importance of finding meaningful and purpose-driven projects to be a part of. It fulfilled me. But the sheer volume of the demands the community had started to take its toll. Whilst it was thrilling to watch the movement grow in numbers and spread – country by country – it felt like it was growing beyond my capacity to manage even with the cooperation of so many volunteers around the world. What had started as a 'passion project' for all of us had become a demanding global operation with no resources to fund it. Operating with 11,000 miles between us – all on a different time zone – every one of us believed in the project but it was becoming something bigger than the growing team of eager volunteers could handle.

Often the strengths of a person or movement can also be the challenges of those same people or movement. No movement or organisation can bring so many people together without challenges or difficulties. #LinkedInLocal was no different. It would be wrong to write this book and the history of #LinkedInLocal without acknowledging and dissecting our response to those challenges.

#LinkedInLocal showed us some of the best of human behaviour. But its success meant that it also showed us some of the most disappointing. Any movement, organisation or community is going to see the best of people and the worst of them. We saw people move off in their own direction, set up their own events under the hashtag and compete with others in their community. We witnessed others attempting to set up similar events – taking the ideas of this one and giving it another name. We saw people organise events with a similar name but completely ignoring the values. These events were sometimes exclusive, for profit and open to sales pitches – basically they were networking events as they had always been but under the guise of the movement. Recognised #LinkedInLocal hosts did their best to demonstrate the values and principles and the vast majority remained committed and did what they did for their communities without any expectation of financial gain or boost to career or business. But there were inevitably those who sought to profit from what they saw as a viral success. The best and worst things are often inextricably woven together. The passion and energy from hosts to step up as a community leader was intense. It was that passion that brought so many ideas to the table. But a handful of people could not fathom that the movement was about the people that came and not for the purpose of building their own social currency. We had just one instance where we co-founders chose to remove an individual from the #LinkedInLocal community. A host involved early on with the mentoring decided that they were entitled to take a percentage of the ticket sales their mentees' events made. This behaviour, brought to our attention by several other hosts, was completely outside the #LinkedInLocal values and principles that hosts were asked to adhere to. It also caused stress and confusion for those attending these events. Fortunately, this was the only occasion we were forced to ask someone to leave the community which I think shows how ingrained and treasured the values were among hosts globally. This was crucial to the success of the movement as most of the events were self-regulated. Furthermore, hosts who broke the code often met with little success. For example hosts who were selling or using their mailing list to promote their own services found that the attendance was low at subsequent events. #LinkedinLocal attendees sought out events because they were curious and wanted to be a part a community and were quick to back away when it became clear they were being used for promotion or other business gains.

Then there were the inevitable challenges that arise with human collaboration. There were differences of opinion – hosts argued and refused to work with one another. There were rivalries – one individual would push other hosts out in their location in order to be seen as the central figure for that group. The old adage of 'too many cooks spoil the broth' put pay to some collaborations – too many ideas and too many directions to pull in. Some hosts, not unlike myself, were overwhelmed by what they had taken on. Planning regular, well-run events is time consuming and labour-intensive. They found that they were unable to sustain the work required and were therefore unable to create an ongoing local community.

We'd often have individuals making a grab for 'land rights' or exclusivity over an entire city, town, region or – in some cases – entire states when it came to event organising. Even in larger cities – where there was perhaps room for multiple local events – this was a demand that came up time and time again. We had never sought to trademark the name or the value system so had no means to formally police hosting.

As founders, we always felt collaboration was the answer to this problem and was the approach that was most consistent with the values and principles the movement. We frequently asked that hosts consider joining forces with existing event organisers or consider a point of difference in their events. For example – with a different industry focus and a different audience or they might consider holding the event in another part of the city. In most cities this worked very well. Toronto was a great example of this. Six groups within the city supported one another and often spoke at each other's events. The city was divided geographically, with some localised around colleges or themes such as #NewtoCanada. Another great example was London. Alongside Alex's events there were #LinkedInLocals in other parts of the city, as well as events specifically for young people and for women. Bristol and Bath, two cities very close in proximity in the UK, held events on alternate months. One would host events during the day and the other in the evenings, making the events as accessible as possible for their local communities.

Successful collaborations like these meant that the movement could spread both deep and wide. Width – in the number of countries, cities or attendees. Depth – in the events and communities that impacted smaller or outer suburbs, universities and colleges, as well as create special interest groups. As a result, the entire movement went deeper into the hearts and minds of a city.

The co-founders and I had no idea when we organised those first events that we would find ourselves in positions of leadership of a growing global movement. Subsequently, our leadership style became something we gave careful thought to. It was a conscious decision for the movement to allow hosts to 'think global and act local'. We envisaged a situation where hosts would be able to respond to the needs of their local community, under the global, non-negotiable but broad values and principles we'd espoused with those first events. Our leadership approach was based on the idea that, as long as the values and principles were adhered to, hosts could be left to their own devices unless they reached out for support.

It was hard sometimes for us to tell whether this was the right approach. Our default leadership style had to be one of trust, allowing for some tolerance and leniency within the values we had set out. This leniency allowed for some truly special chapters to arise. A lot could have gone wrong but our mentoring process, whilst not flawless, largely meant we were able to create a chapter model that was consistent and continued to draw so many people to it. That leadership style was rooted in what I felt was morally right. I saw myself as a guardian for the name and what people felt it stood for. But because we had limited resources we had to build the host community based on trust. Micro-managing hosts was not an option, nor would it have enabled so many groups to grow and thrive. That we were able to retain the integrity of the values of the movement on such a global scale, is testament to the community sharing those strong core values, communicating them effectively, and attracting the right people to help spread the idea. In this way the values curated the movement, and the user experience.

A Corporate Conundrum

Ever since the first #LinkedInLocal event took place in 2017 there was a question on many people's minds – including my own; how would the LinkedIn corporation react to the movement and the impact it was having? LinkedIn is a large corporation, with headquarters in Sunnyvale, California, and over 9,000 employees. Since December 2016 it has been a wholly owned subsidiary of Microsoft.

Since the very first events, we as founders and mentors were careful to follow the advice in the LinkedIn user agreement. We were continually communicating to users that we were just a community of keen LinkedIn users and in no way formally affiliated with the company. We advised hosts to communicate the same message about their events and to not use the official LinkedIn logo. However, we wanted to work with LinkedIn and made several attempts to connect and start conversations with the right people at the company. This was largely unsuccessful – no one at the corporation seemed to know who could discuss something that had so quickly become global and was so far out of their usual jurisdiction.

At the same time, the demands of the movement were becoming more complex. Larger venues were required and these were more expensive and required insurance. Individual hosting groups in many cities wanted to ensure they could operate formally for tax purposes and to raise money for charities as a formal organisation.

Our intention, taking into account the host feedback and the time we were personally putting into #LinkedInLocal, was to centrally organise, facilitate and provide resources to the community. We considered crowdfunding but ruled it out as asking for money at the time didn't feel consistent with the community values. We decided to use the learning to develop a central organisation (LocalX) to ensure that our time on the project could be justified, and endeavour to use our expertise to monetise our learning, offering consulting on community facilitation, activation, management and development.

We finally spoke to someone at LinkedIn in April 2018, eleven months after the first event. At that point, events were taking place in more than 250 cities, 34 countries and the host community was 450 strong. LinkedIn approached us to discuss the movement based on a Forbes article request. Forbes had approached LinkedIn wanting to publish an article about how users were using the platform to organise and meet their network offline. The article never came to fruition, but it did open a dialogue with decision makers in the product team at LinkedIn. That same month, we later learned, LinkedIn formally trademarked the name LinkedInLocal.

In initial conversations with LinkedIn their feedback was positive and they indicated that they wanted to support the content coming out of the events. There was even discussion about a #LinkedInLocal video filter to be rolled out to hosts to use at the events, however this never took off and was only rolled out to approximately six users.

There were further calls, but the tone changed over time. Their interest and feedback evolved and seemed to be focused more on brand and logo protection than about content, potential features or support for the movement and the work of the hosts. We provided ideas about how LinkedIn and the #LinkedInLocal community could work together. We suggested that #LinkedInLocal could be a part of 'LinkedIn for Good', a social impact arm of LinkedIn which worked with charities to encourage development and learning. We suggested that they could utilise #LinkedInLocal as a way to truly connect the corporation with the user. They could use the community to test and gain feedback on new features – a non-financial way to reward hosts. They could suggest topics and panel discussions on themes that they were keen to explore. They could help create a central place for users to find #LinkedInLocal events, not just in their own city but those happening in locations they were travelling to. We suggested that LinkedIn look at #LinkedInLocal in a similar way to #linkedinlife, a widely used hashtag and Instagram account utilised by LinkedIn employees to share why they love working for LinkedIn. The #Linkedinlocal hashtag could be promoted to their users as a way to share why they loved the platform and to share the impact stories. We wanted to stress that this was an opportunity for the company to emerge as a major player in the online to offline space, to demonstrate how technology can be used for good and to create some truly wonderful and authentic marketing messages of how their platform was impacting others. We felt it could be a valuable way to increase engagement on the platform. We also knew that LinkedIn was benefitting from increased user engagement as a result of the events. A social media platform's success is not only measured by the number of individual accounts but also by how engaged its users are. The success of the events meant more users were logging in to share varied and authentic content and enrich the platform. Event attendees told us that they were encouraged by the events to create more content on the platform and use it for more than simply job hunting. The content being created was varied. As an example, Alex shared a post about her mental health, which was viewed by around 80,000 people. The videos and photos that came after the events were always inspiring for others, gaining high view numbers and engaging comments. It highlighted why so many continued to join and remain involved in the movement – the need for face to face connection beyond the digital world.

Despite all our efforts at driving these ideas and potential benefits to the company, LinkedIn's main aim seemed to be protecting their brand. In March 2019 they issued terms for all LinkedIn users regarding the use of the hashtag and the name, LinkedInLocal. The new terms of use officially allowed use of the company logo and name at #LinkedInLocal events. This was extremely positive as it was something we had been asking for permission for since the early conversations. Events could no longer be co-branded, but users were encouraged to set up their own websites for their groups allowing for the use of the LinkedIn name in the url which had previously not been allowed.

However, the terms drawn up by LinkedIn included no reference to the values and principles that the movement had been based on and now operated under. Events were no longer required to be not-for-profit and pitch-free. For us, this meant that the heart of the movement had been removed. It was a big blow for us and one that signalled a huge change. None of us felt able to continue to drive the movement under the current terms and conditions. The new terms meant we had lost our original purpose, to authentically connect people beyond the profiles in a way that valued others without selling. The new terms excluded many of the reasons the movement had been so appealing. The river that was #LinkedInLocal had reached its end and we would now need to let it drift into the sea.

My personal response to the terms when I first saw them was one of disbelief – but also relief. I was exhausted and to finally have a formal answer to our questions from LinkedIn was something at least. I'd been feeling for a while that I could no longer carry the weight of the community we'd created. Now we had our answer from the company and we could move on.

But I also had a deep sense of responsibility for this community. I wanted to find a way to recognise the hosts for all of their hard work and create some kind of lasting legacy for what we had collectively achieved. LinkedIn had failed to grasp the commitment of hosts, their love of the platform, and the hosts' connection to the values. In my mind, they failed to see the impact the movement was having on their users and missed an opportunity to leverage that and build upon its stories and viral growth. Stepping away from the host community was one of the hardest things I've had to do in my career. But – for my own family, for my own sanity – there was only one decision to make, to move aside and let the community grow as LinkedIn wished it.

In October 2019, in an attempt to support ongoing events, LinkedIn relaunched their events functionality as a tool for any event organiser to use to promote their events. Re-introducing this meant hosts were finally able to promote events on the platform, but it didn't make community management any simpler for hosts.

It's not unusual for large corporations to struggle to respond effectively or efficiently to innovation, and the growth of #LinkedInLocal had been extremely fast and unexpected. Every individual we spoke to at LinkedIn was a huge supporter of the idea and what we had achieved but, as a corporation, the response was driven by the legal aspects only. Corporations, in fact all businesses, spend an enormous amount on PR, marketing and communications. By anyone's assessment #LinkedInLocal was soft marketing and corporate responsibility all rolled into one. Swish felt let down by the company – they were benefitting indirectly through the name from the optics of the great work happening around the world but they seemed unable or unwilling to fully support it. He said he felt that it could've been ten times bigger with even minimal support from LinkedIn. He said, 'I do hope that in five to ten years, LinkedIn looks back and they realise that they missed out on a massive opportunity. Especially given the fact that today, more than ever in the online world we live in, we constantly seek offline experiences. #LinkedInLocal could have just been that vehicle that they could have ridden on to get there.'

Alex said, 'In the end we had to stand by what we believed in, by the values that held our #LinkedInLocal Family together. And I wonder, what would've happened if they had helped us nurture that beating heart we'd discovered amongst the grey, concrete, glass skyscrapers and high rises. Perhaps the corporate world wasn't ready to be human.'

LinkedIn's core marketing message is 'Connecting to opportunity.' #LinkedInLocal was a movement that brought people together and really embodied that idea. It was organised in a manner that put the person first, rather than a business. At the time the new terms were issued in March 2019, #LinkedInLocal had reach into 92 countries and 650 towns and cities. It was a network that could create change, build bridges, tear down walls and cross borders in an unprecedented way. In a world where online to offline is emerging as a whole new industry in itself, I often wonder 'what if…?'

Conclusion

This book was intended to bring together the stories of the #LinkedInLocal Family to demonstrate what can happen when people come together to do something good for others.

We wanted to share the extraordinary experience we were part of. From one post about a catch up over coffee to events in 92 countries, over 650 towns and cities, with more than 1,000 hosts, #LinkedInLocal was a hashtag that changed the world for the better in less than two years.

Although it is now under the guidance of LinkedIn through the issue of the 2019 terms, #LinkedInLocal continues to provide so much to so many communities, and more and more hosts are flocking to it daily. The #LinkedInLocal river now feeds into an ocean and it has carved a permanent path in our social landscape – both online and offline.

The story of #LinkedInLocal is a story about the power of social media. It's a story for current and future generations to help them understand how and what social media can be used for. In a world where an individual sense of worth can be based on the number of likes or followers, this story shows that there are ways in which we can focus our relationships more on interactions rather than transactions. It is an example of humans disrupting technology and using it to go to the very heart of what we all crave – a connection to those around us.

#LinkedInLocal also showed the importance of nurturing offline connections. It shows how we can blend our online and offline networks and have more thoughtful conversations. The human race has some pretty complex problems to solve, and we need real world solutions. The likelihood of solving these is far greater if we can understand other people's perspectives and ideas. Listening to each other means we can develop ways to foster more tolerant societies. If we prioritise online connection, we risk operating in filter bubbles where we only interact with people like us, where we are only exposed to information we want to see. Our world gets smaller. You can't fake offline connection. That connection is real, and it's core to who we are.

#LinkedInLocal was also an example of authentic marketing and finding another channel in which to share a brand's message. The way advertising and marketing has evolved has eroded people's trust and as human beings we are now looking to people or brands with a level of authenticity and social responsibility. Fake news, being bombarded with an alarming number of advertisements, and growing social isolation has increased our affinity for more genuine messages and connections.

It also married technology and human connection in one place. As Quddus Pourshafie so eloquently put it, '#LinkedinLocal showed the power of human connection in a way that was unique. Instead of pushing for human connection at the cost of technology, it did so while embracing technology by creating an organic cycle of online to offline interactions that demonstrated equal value and utility. This made it clear that beyond #LinkedinLocal there was a calling and the capacity to create cohesion between the human aspect of community and the vast capability of technology platforms. #LinkedinLocal is a precursor to the growth of communities beyond just charitable and non-profit groups. It demonstrated how communities will be the future driver of business, aligning the values of corporations with its employees while also seamlessly integrating their products and services with consumers lifestyle and choices.'

One thing we can all learn from #LinkedInLocal is that there are a lot of people willing to create change both locally and globally when they are united behind a common cause or set of values. What we achieved together as a collective touched so many lives, and it was done with minimal resources. Through the sheer drive and desire for change human beings have the capacity to come together and create better spaces, communities and companies that can have a positive impact on our societies. Sometimes all it takes to begin this change is conscious leadership.

Founder Reflections

In the words of Alex Galviz:

'It all started with an idea, and four people of which I was one. We had one mission, to build a community of like-minded people that could help each other, empower each other, inspire each other. A community that everyone was welcome in, no matter what age, race and ethnicity. Titles were left at the door and business cards had zero value. You went in as yourself and hopefully you went back into your corporate jobs a little more human.

It was a community built on human connections created in what is a very cold, corporate world. We found you, you found us and we united in our passions. As I walked across the world to meet you all in person, door after door was opened, I was welcomed into houses, into cities, into groups that were foreign when I entered and family when I departed. '

In the words of Erik Eklund:

'There are friends in strangers and discoveries in adventures. Unexpected events bring people together, intimate moments connect people in the most human of ways. What's the difference between interaction and connection? The intimacy of the conversation.

There are so many stories and the legacy this movement has left reaches far and wide. I thank you – all of you who reminded the world what it is to be human and that trusting relationships are easy to build when we choose to open up and come together as human beings. Are we not one species after all?'

In the words of Swish Goswami:

'As online communities grow and more people come onto social media, my hope is that we never forget the value of connecting with others in person. It was what I loved about #LinkedInLocal – the focus on bringing people from the online world through to offline experiences that could unite them around issues.

Now more than ever, we need people to know they are not alone in their journey and we need them to know that there are people who go through the same struggles and issues they do. That's what #LinkedInLocal has done for people and I've been proud to be a part of it.'

In the words of Anna McAfee:

'I will forever be touched by the stories from this river, by the drops it's left behind and the changes in the world it's made – however big or small. I can only hope the same for many of those involved and the readers of this book.

We all have the power within us to provide a sense

of belonging to other human beings. We all deserve to be seen, heard and lifted up. We all, as individuals, have the capacity to seek those with less advantages than us and to make things better. To an individual this can feel daunting but, as a collective, we can build a better sense of what's around us, our needs and our society as we look to the future.

I truly believe we need curated communities to activate that, to nurture that drive, to be its catalyst, to create momentum. Only together can we try and make sense of what's in front of us.

#LinkedInLocal is a movement, a revolution and a culture. It has ultimately been a vehicle to express ourselves, and show what it means to be human. It's been a privilege to be a part of it, and to have guided that river's direction, even if just for a short time.'

In Memorium
Mohammad Asadi Lari

These are the words of Andrew Griffiths, friend and co-host of Mohammad's first #LinkedInLocal event.

'I met Mohammad shortly after I arrived in Vancouver. He had told me that he would be holding his first event three weeks after my arrival in Canada. When he told me the venue he'd secured I was blown away. Mohammad was on the Youth Advisory Board of the iconic Science World on the Vancouver waterfront. He had loads of other organisations and interests that he could've used this contact for, but he told me he'd asked the President of Science World if he could use their venue for a #LinkedInLocal event. He saw it as a great way to bring young people into the #LinkedInLocal community. He was drawn to it because of the well-defined community values. Two weeks before the event I was happy to attend a viewing of the venue with Mohammad and finally meet him face to face. I agreed to help him organise the event.

We managed to secure some amazing speakers, caterers and videographers, Zain Gaziani, then a community manager for speaker Gary Vee and based in Seattle, was our keynote speaker.

Yonden Sherpa, became out third co-host. Yonden had moved to Toronto and flew in just for the event. Mohammad and Yonden each chaired one of the panels and I chaired the event as a whole. More than 150 people – CEOs, academics and young people – attended and it was incredible.

My friendship with Mohammad was forged by fire. It was an intense, amazing and fulfilling baptism. That event at Science World will stay with me forever. The energy, the camaraderie were proof of what can happen when people want to do something great for their community.

Mohammad was a natural leader right from the get-go. At 16, Mohammad moved from his home in Tehran to Canada, with just his younger sister Zeynab – leaving their parents behind. He told me he had struggled to connect with other students. One of his teachers suggested he should set up a science club and invite others along as a way to get to know them better. He did. In true Mohammad style he brought his vision to life and, working with a like-minded person he met in Toronto, the STEM Fellowship was born. The Fellowship grew to cover all of Canada, arranging mentorships, grants and competitions. Mohammad was 17 years old when he started this and his sister Zeynab, then 15, led on the HR systems and processes behind the scenes.

Mohammad also became a youth advisor for The Canadian Commission for the UNESCO, the Canadian Institutes for Health Research, the Canadian Red Cross, Science World British Columbia, the non-partisan, civic engagement group 'Apathy is Boring' and the World Economic Forum. He was vice-president of global health with the University of Toronto Medical Society and helped to advocate on international health, aid and equity. In February 2019 he did a TEDx Talk about the ways in which we can empower youth.

He received, in his short but impactful life numerous national and international scientific Olympiad medals; a 3M National Student Fellowship; a Governor General's bronze academic medal; a University of British Columbia *Faces of Today* Leadership award; a Society for Scholarly Publishing Fellowship and was a 2018 Royal Bank of Canada (RBC) Top 25 Immigrant Finalist.

Mohammad radiated kindness and tirelessly volunteered. He supported friends and colleagues and he brought his ambitious ideas to life. Of all of the young leaders I have ever had the pleasure of meeting Mohammad's capacity to unite people and to make things happen made him stand out. I thought there was every chance he would end up the leader of a country. Above all else he was a good friend.'

On January 8th, 2020 Mohammad Asadi Lari (aged 23) was killed in the Ukraine International Airlines Flight PS752 which came down just outside of Tehran, Iran, with his sister Zeynab Asadi Lari (aged 21).

Acknowledgements

In addition to the founders, there were a team of people crucial to building this community. The host mentors played an important role in introducing and supporting new hosts and maintaining the quality of the experience in this global community. We would like to give recognition and a special thanks to those who volunteered their time to provide support, mentor others and make this community thrive.

Scott Berty, a sales and growth specialist, is a #LinkedInLocal host based in Toronto, Canada. Scott ran weekly mentoring calls for over a year for many hosts around the globe.

Gregory Caillol, a digital marketing specialist in Montpellier began mentoring in France and other French-speaking cities also stepped in to help in Europe, UK and North America.

Lila Smith, a communications speaker and trainer, based in Dallas, ran mentoring calls to help meet demand from the US.

Matt Gagnon, a life coach and host in Austin Texas, played a big part in events in Texas, as a speaker and an attendee. Matt stepped in to host mentoring calls for the US region.

Raegan Fatouros, a general manager of a heavy machinery company and a host based in Toronto, Canada, helped new hosts in the US and Canada.

Andrew Griffiths, a community builder and host in London and Vancouver, helped hosts get started in the UK, US and Canada.

Jillian Bullock, a LinkedIn expert and host in Sydney stepped up to help support Australasia.

Priya Dhawan, a senior manager in marketing and communications and lead host in Pune, India assisted many South Asian hosts in getting started.

Evelyn Andrade, a vice president of human resources, speaker and also co-host in Fort Lauderdale, assisted Central and South America with calls in Spanish.

Marie Quinquis a project leader and host in Toulouse joined the mentoring team to run calls in French, largely to meet the demand for growth in French-speaking Africa as well as in France.

Greg Cooper, a LinkedIn trainer based in Bristol started mentoring hosts in the UK, having one run one of the UK's most successful #LinkedInLocal communities for a year.

Krista Mollion, a business coach, leader and host in San Francisco, USA ran monthly calls for the members of the host community to communicate as a group and exchange ideas.

We would like to thank the many people who submitted their articles and stories to be included in this book. There were so many that we couldn't include them all, but thank you all so much for sharing your stories with us.

Thanks

I am indebted to the people who trusted us enough with their personal and professional journeys to contribute to this project. Thank you also to the many people that were involved either as hosts or attendees of #LinkedInLocal around the world who continually inspired this movement.

Firstly, to my co-author Nicole Johnston for her guidance, belief and vision of what we could achieve together. To Caroline Goldsmith, who was a dream editor, making my words more impactful than I ever could. Her suggestions and encouragement helped us enormously.

For their additional assistance in bringing the book project together I extend my gratitude to Tamar Hela, Quddus Pourshafie, Anthony English, Katrina Ramage, Alexandra Galviz, Marlon De Cruz, Laci Glenn, and Lila Smith.

As ever, I am immensely grateful to my parents for teaching me to listen, to tell stories and to acknowledge mental health struggles (my own, and others).

To my children, Orla and Hugh, for teaching me what is actually important in life, and to Gerard, for everything.

Anna McAfee

First and foremost thanks to my greatest friend, supporter and endlessly patient proofreader – my husband, Chris Johnston; to the most fantastic, encouraging and excellent editor I have ever worked with – Caroline Goldsmith; to my brilliant friend who, in an insane moment, agreed to proofread the book and set me straight on what wasn't working Rachel Marangazov and to my co-author, Anna McAfee, who valiantly leapt into the world of writing to tell hundreds of inspiring stories in one. Taking care and responsibility for the stories of so many is a challenge that not many would take on, let alone in their first book. Last, but definitely not least, to the unsung heroes of this movement – the partners (professional and personal) and families of the co-founders, the global team, the host mentors and the hosts – who gave their time, effort, support and kept the rest of our lives working while we all threw ourselves into something we believed in. It couldn't have happened without all of you!

Nicole Johnston

About the Authors

Anna McAfee is a community educator and LinkedIn Trainer, and is driven to help individuals and businesses to build better and more authentic connections in a digital world. She lives in Coffs Harbour, Australia with her husband and two children. This is her first book.

You can contact Anna at www.annamcafee.com.au

Formerly an advisor to senior government ministers in the UK and Australia **Nicole Johnston** is an author, ghostwriter and writing coach. She writes fiction and non-fiction. Her third novel is due out at the end of 2020. She hails from Perth in Australia but now lives in a leafy suburb in southeast London with her husband.

You can contact Nicole at www.writingtribe.com.

Endnotes

[1] https://www.digitaltrends.com/features/the-history-of-social-networking/

[2] https://www.pewinternet.org/2014/12/30/technologys-impact-on-workers/

[3] https://www.idbs.com/resource-center/12-tips-for-increasing-workplace-productivity-with-technology/

[4] https://www.entrepreneur.com/article/274388

[5] https://reports.weforum.org/human-implications-of-digital-media-2016/benefits-and-opportunities/

[6] https://www.scientificamerican.com/article/why-we-are-wired-to-connect/

[7] https://www.un.org/development/desa/disabilities/issues/mental-health-and-development-html

[8] https://news.harvard.edu/gazette/story/2017/04/over-nearly-80-years-harvard-study-has-been-showing-how-to-live-a-healthy-and-happy-life/

[9] https://www.globalpsa.com/internet-of-logistics-summit-connecting-communities-enabling-transformation/

Printed in Poland
by Amazon Fulfillment
Poland Sp. z o.o., Wrocław

62181821R00115